Workplace Grace

Other Resources by Bill Peel

What God Does When Men Lead

Discover Your Destiny (coauthored with Kathy Peel)

Discover Your Destiny (eight-session video series)

Living in the Lab Without Smelling Like a Cadaver

Living in the Lions' Den Without Being Eaten

The Saline Solution (coauthored with Walt Larimore)

What God Does When Men Pray

Where Is Moses When We Need Him? (coauthored with Kathy Peel)

The Busy Couple's Guide to Sharing the Work and Joy (contributor)

Marriage and Family Resources at www.FamilyManager.com

Workplace, Evangelism, and Men's Ministry Resources at www.24SevenFaith.com

Other Resources by Walt Larimore

10 Essentials of Happy, Healthy People: Becoming and Staying Highly Healthy

God's Design for the Highly Healthy Child

God's Design for the Highly Healthy Teen

Alternative Medicine: The Christian Handbook (coauthored with Dónal O'Mathúna)

Bryson City Tales: Stories of a Doctor's First Year of Practice in the Smoky Mountains

Bryson City Seasons: More Tales of a Doctor's Practice in the Smoky Mountains

Bryson City Secrets: Even More Tales of a Small-Town Doctor in the Smoky Mountains

The Saline Solution: Sharing Christ in a Busy Practice (coauthored with Bill Peel)

Lintball Leo's Not-So-Stupid Questions About Your Body

SuperSized Kids: How to Protect Your Child from the Obesity Threat
(coauthored with Cheryl Flynt and Steve Halladay)

His Brain, Her Brain: How Divinely Designed Differences Can Strengthen Your
Marriage (coauthored with Barb Larimore)

The Honeymoon of Your Dreams: How to Plan a Romantic Life Together
(coauthored with Susan Crockett)

Why A.D.H.D. Doesn't Mean Disaster
(coauthored with Dennis Swanburg and Diane Passno)

Time Scene Investigators: The Gabon Virus (a novel)
(coauthored with Paul McCusker)

Christian Health Blog at www.DrWalt.com/blog

Christian Health Resources at www.DrWalt.com

Autographed Books available at www.DrWalt.com/books

Workplace Grace

BECOMING A SPIRITUAL INFLUENCE AT WORK

Bill Peel & Walt Larimore

Previously titled Going Public with Your Faith

ZONDERVAN®

ZONDERVAN.com/
AUTHORTRACKER
follow your favorite authors

ZONDERVAN

Workplace Grace
Copyright © 2003, 2010 by William Carr Peel and Walt Larimore

Previously titled as *Going Public with Your Faith*

This title is also available as a Zondervan ebook. Visit www.zondervan.com/ebooks.

This title is also available in a Zondervan audio edition. Visit www.zondervan.fm.

Requests for information should be addressed to:

Zondervan, *Grand Rapids, Michigan 49530*

Library of Congress Cataloging-in-Publication Data

Peel, William Carr.
    Workplace grace : becoming a spiritual influence at work / William Carr Peel and
Walt Larimore. — 1st ed.
      p. cm.
    Includes bibliographical references.
    ISBN 978-0-310-32972-5
    1. Evangelistic work. 2. Witness bearing (Christianity). 3. Work — Religious
aspects — Christianity. I. Larimore, Walter L. II. Title.
BV3790.P44   2003
269'.2 — dc21
                                               2003008437

Cover design: Jody Langley
Interior design: Ben Fetterley

Printed in the United States of America

10 11 12 13 14 15 /DCI/ 22 21 20 19 18 17 16 15 14 13 12 11 10 9 8 7 6 5 4 3 2 1

To Bill Garrison,
who taught me that most of God's heroes are in the workplace
—Bill Peel

To Bill Judge,
who mentored me in life and faith
and taught me how they work together in the workplace
—Walt Larimore

CONTENTS

ACKNOWLEDGMENTS

From cover to cover, this book has been influenced by many people. Jim Petersen of the Navigators and Bill Kraftson of Search Ministries started us thinking in a new way about our own spiritual impact. The writings of Joe Aldridge, George Barna, John Fischer, C. S. Lewis, Rebecca Pippert, and Dorothy Sayers helped shape our philosophy.

The Christian Medical and Dental Associations, sponsor of "The Saline Solution," made it possible for us to teach health care professionals to share their faith in the workplace. We sincerely appreciate the confidence of David Stevens and Gene Rudd and the support of Wayne Sanders, David Bushong, Sarah Matthews, Barbara Snap, and the entire staff at CMDA.

Thank you to the ten thousand-plus graduates of "The Saline Solution" course worldwide. Your helpful feedback and kind encouragement prompted us to translate the course principles for use in the nonmedical workplace.

Thanks also go to Cindy Lambert, Dirk Buursma, Stan Gundry, Scott Bolinder, Sue Brower, Lyn Cryderman, and the Zondervan team for believing *Workplace Grace* deserved to be published.

Personally, we are grateful for the many people who have influenced (and continue to influence) our lives. Dan Johnson's passion to distribute God's truth in creative ways to the world has inspired me (Bill). The commitment of Ambassador Joe Rodgers to integrate faith and work drives me and many others to do the same. Longtime friends David and Kathryn Waldrep incessantly serve God by serving others; they are a shining example of faith at work on a daily basis. And I sincerely value the prayers and support of Bill Counts, Reagan Dixon, and the other elders at Fellowship Bible Church who have encouraged me to think about faith outside the four walls of our church.

Dr. John Hartman deserves special thanks as my (Walt's) partner in medical practice for over sixteen years. John and I hammered out the principles contained in this book through trial and error at our medical practice in Kissimmee, Florida. God has used many pastors to impact my life, including Donald Tabb, Larry Miller, Mac Bare, Ken Hicks, Nathan Blackwell, and Chris Taylor.

We also wish to acknowledge the following business leaders who provided interviews for both the written and audio versions of this book: Jack Alexander, cochairman of Geronimo Fund; Anne Beiler, founder and CEO of Auntie Anne's, Inc.; Larry Collett, executive vice president of Cass Commercial Bank; Jack DeWitt, president of Request Foods; James Lindemann, executive vice president of Emerson Electric; Norm Miller, chairman of the board for Interstate Battery System of America, Inc.; Merrill Oster, chairman of Oster Communications & Oster Dow Jones Commodity News; John Seiple, managing director and COO of ProLogis Operating System; Marvin (Skip) Schoenhals, chairman, president, and CEO of WSFS Financial Corporation; Jose Zeilstra, vice president, Global Finance.

Both of us are indebted to our life partners, Kathy Peel and Barb Larimore. They make our lives rich, and they challenge us to be our best. It's a great privilege to live and work with them.

Heartfelt hugs go to John, Joel, and James Peel and to Kate and Scott Larimore. To be a father is an unspeakable blessing, and we have no greater joy than to see that our children are walking in the truth. Thanks for allowing us to practice our faith on and with you.

—Bill Peel, Dallas, Texas

—Walt Larimore, Colorado Springs, Colorado

INTRODUCTION

"I want my life to count. I don't want to look back at the end and think I wasted it."

Most of us have heard this sentiment expressed many times. Many of us, the authors included, have expressed it ourselves. The desire to make a positive difference—to be significant—before God is a healthy desire. Those in the church, evangelicals in particular, define this significance largely in terms of their efforts to share the gospel—to spread the Word, to see others at home and abroad come to faith in Jesus Christ.

Unfortunately, few have experienced much success in this area of their Christian lives. Efforts to share Christ seem uncomfortable, awkward, ineffective, perhaps even counterproductive. The formulas and methods for sharing the gospel seem mechanical, unrealistic. They may look good on paper, but they just don't seem to be working. Thus many, despite their desire to carry out this biblical responsibility, have simply given up.

If you have questions about how to share your faith, this book will help. You will see how the seemingly insignificant words you speak and actions you take can have great significance before God and in the lives of the people you encounter.

WITNESS THE WAYS

As you will soon see, our focus is on our culture's ripest mission field—the workplace. You will encounter others who have gone public in their places of work whose testimonies can instruct and inspire. One such person is George. I (Bill) sat across the table from George as he finished the paperwork for the purchase of my wife's fiftieth-birthday present. He is a jeweler of Lebanese descent whose grandfatherly personality, exotic accent, and love of Jesus make my heart smile every time I visit his store. I asked, "George, what's the favorite part of your job?" He quickly replied, "Helping young couples find a beautiful ring that is just right for them." He explained how, as he does his work, he looks for opportunities to impart some small bit of biblical wisdom about relationships. He pulled out a note from his desk drawer and read a few lines a young bride had recently written:

> Thank you so much for helping us find the beautiful ring and making it possible for us to purchase it. Of all the salespeople who helped us, you seemed to really care about us. And thank you for the advice about marriage. Dick and I have decided we need to find a church to attend. Thanks for your encouragement.

And there is John, a caretaker. Before leaving on a business trip to England, John's boss gave him final instructions: "Take good care of my family, John." The graying caretaker smiled and said, "I will, and I'll pray for your success." The executive paused, looked back, and said, "John, I don't know what I'd do without you. There's no one on this island I trust more than you."

It hadn't always been that way. A great sea of mistrust separates the cultures that John and his employer come from. One was raised in a privileged environment, the son of six generations of plantation owners on the island of Barbados; the other was the son of slaves. When John began working for his wealthy boss ten years ago, he was charged with maintaining the perimeter of the property. He was not allowed to go anywhere near the house. Each year, John's hard work and godly character earned him more responsibility. Today John oversees the entire property, entrusted with not only the house and grounds but also with the well-being of the family when his boss is away on business. John told me he prays daily for this man and his family. "God has allowed me to win my way into his house. Now I pray that God will open their hearts so they'll come to know Jesus."

These followers of Jesus in the workplace are passionate about their faith. They love to talk to people about Jesus. But their motive is not to proselytize. Rather it is to discover what God is already doing in someone's life and to join that effort. It is to show Jesus to those with whom they work, not to sell Jesus or force him on others. It is to help others become new creations, not to coerce people to "change religions."

A New Way to Look at Evangelism

Our proposition is simple: For most Christians these days, the workplace—not the church or a foreign mission field—is the primary setting for effective kingdom work. We believe this proposition to be both biblically and historically true. When the church has allowed people to set their focus inside the four walls, it has tended to dwindle in size. But when the church has launched people outward into the world, encouraging them to express publicly their faith, it has invariably grown. The early church is a prime example. It grew from a handful of disciples in the AD 30s to over half a million people by the end of the first century. This growth didn't occur as a result of the proliferation of full-time missionaries; it happened because ordinary followers of Jesus took their faith to the workplace and lived it out in their ordinary everyday encounters. Early Christians chatted about the gospel in bakeries, shops, marketplaces, and barracks. From the dusty streets of Jerusalem to the soggy outposts of the British Isles, these early followers of Jesus spread the gospel gladly and with an enthusiasm that could never be produced by wage or sense of duty.

At times, God provides other avenues for spreading the gospel. But we contend that the primary historical means God uses to spread the Good News and extend the influence of faith is to "send it to work" with ordinary people. This was our premise in 1995 when we teamed up to develop "The Saline Solution," with the goal of teaching doctors how to talk about their faith with their patients. Ironically, neither of us considered himself a gifted evangelist. Both of us have had thorough training to aggressively present the gospel message to people we didn't know. And even though we had a great desire to share our faith, we broke into a cold sweat when faced with the opportunity to talk about Jesus with non-Christians. What emerged from our collaboration was serious business—a new model of evangelism, a model of spiritual influence that doctors who live under intense time pressure and significant ethical limitations can use every day with every patient. As we taught this approach to doctors, many of whom have a deep passion for spiritual impact, we regularly heard the same three comments: (1) "I feel a load of guilt has been taken off my shoulders," (2) "I can do this!" and (3) "You need to adapt this for other professions besides health care."

This is our goal for this book. We believe the *workplace grace* approach to offering spiritual truth to a lost world is biblical. We believe it will change the way Christians view evangelism and also the way non-Christians view Christians.

As we examined both Scripture and our own experience, we stumbled on a concept that is often ignored by modern evangelistic methods: Evangelism is not an event but a process. That is, evangelism is less about imparting a set of facts about God and humankind and asking a person to make a decision to receive Jesus as Savior on the spot than it is about a process—usually a prolonged process—that begins by preparing or *cultivating* someone's heart to receive that message.

To put it another way, evangelism is organic, not mechanical. Interestingly, the Bible consistently chooses an agrarian model to describe evangelism. Evangelism, after all, is a process comparable to growing a crop: cultivation + planting → harvest. It takes time to cultivate a relationship in which seeds of biblical truth can be planted and can grow, resulting in an eventual harvest of eternal life.

We believe that the bubble has burst for an aggressive, nonrelational approach to evangelism. It's time to go back to the farm for our model. Like growing a crop, evangelism takes intentional work over an extended period of time. There's nothing instant about it. For people who love to "close the deal," such "preliminaries" may seem like a waste of time. But we strongly believe that people today have no more desire to hear from a stranger about how to receive eternal life than they do to invest all their money in the next cold-call stock tip. Skepticism about Christian faith is as prominent today as it has ever been. This is a significant barrier to belief that must be recognized, addressed, and overcome if we expect people to come to faith. To do so takes time.

The journey of faith consists of a multitude of small, incremental decisions regarding spiritual realities. Thus the greatest privilege in the world—being part of someone's journey to Jesus—can begin with something as simple as having a cup of coffee with a colleague, listening compassionately when a customer shares why she's had a rough week, or doing something beyond the call of duty for a boss or employee who's under stress. As you read and interact with the ideas in this book, you will see that small actions and simple attempts to serve others in the course of everyday life have a bigger impact than the "spiritual interruptions" we sometimes seek to orchestrate out of a sense of guilt.

You will also discover that, although you play an important role, it is ultimately *God* who is at work behind the scenes to create opportunities for meaningful discussions about spiritual topics. Our job as God's representatives is not to try to "start a fire in the rain" but to discover where he is already at work and to pour fuel on that fire.

We regularly meet men and women who do not consider themselves evangelists by any stretch of the imagination. Yet they love God deeply and want their lives to count for his kingdom. Our prayer is that you, our readers, will not only recognize the incredible influence you can have right where you are but that you will also experience the unparalleled joy of seeing the people with whom you work come to know Jesus. Oh, and we'd also love to see you set free from guilt and learn to say, with God-given confidence, "I can do this!"

SPIRITUAL ECONOMICS

In 1921, President Franklin Delano Roosevelt was stricken with polio, a disease he struggled with until his death in April 1945. On the tenth anniversary of FDR's death, Dr. Jonas Salk announced that the polio vaccine he had developed was ready for use by the general public. Over thirty years later, in the late 1980s, thousands of doses of oral polio vaccine were being stored in drug company refrigerators. Yet hundreds of thousands of polio cases were still being reported around the globe. The supply was plentiful. The problem was a failure of distribution.

In stepped Rotary International, which set a lofty goal—to eradicate polio from the world. The organization raised more than $200 million to buy enough vaccine to meet the entire global need. But they, too, confronted the same massive problem—distribution. Working in conjunction with the World Health Organization, Rotarians developed a strategy that called for identifying the neediest countries and designating "national vaccination days." Thousands of health officials and volunteers vaccinated entire countries against polio in a matter of days or weeks. By 2001, only 500 cases of polio were reported worldwide. By addressing the challenge of distribution, the Rotarians have saved thousands from premature death or disability.

Basic economic principles revolve around supply, demand, and distribution. A business enterprise may have abundant capital, solid management, and a worthy product. None of it will matter even a little bit if the enterprise cannot address the challenge of *distribution*. No matter how strong the demand or how abundant the supply in the warehouse, if the enterprise cannot get the product into the hands of the consumer, its demise is inevitable.

Many of the world's problems are a result of failure to meet the challenge of distribution. While the granaries in many developed nations overflow, millions go to bed hungry each night. We've all read the accounts of how rival factions in various Third World countries prevent grain from reaching starving people. The problem is *distribution*—figuring out how to bridge the gap between abundant resources and desperate demand. Tons of much-needed food and water sat in warehouses in Umm Qasr in the spring of 2003 while Iraqis went without basic necessities because Iraq's distribution system was virtually nonexistent.

One of the key components to America's prosperity is its distribution system, that is, our ability to identify a need, develop a product or service to meet the need, and then deliver it to the customer quickly and efficiently. Although Sam Walton (the richest man in America until his death in 1992) has been called a retailer, the true key to the success of Wal-Mart is automated distribution. It efficiently delivers goods to its more than 3,200 facilities in the United States and passes on the savings to its more than 100 million weekly customers.[1]

THE SPIRITUAL CHALLENGE

This same dynamic applies to the realm of spiritual resources. All over the world, people are looking as never before for spiritual answers and resources. As human solutions continue to fail, more and more people are seeking divine help. Vaclav Havel, president of the Czech Republic, has said, "Communism has left a vacuum in the hearts of men." Stories of spiritual hunger from the former Soviet bloc pour into the West.

But by no means do the spiritually oppressed in the former Soviet Union have a corner on spiritual need. In 1995 researcher and futurist George Barna estimated that the number of people in the United States who do not have a relationship with Jesus would reach 235 million by 2000,[2] making the U.S. home to the world's fourth largest non-Christian population.

Americans are not so much antispiritual as they are indifferent to religious institutions. In 2000, Barna reported that the number of unchurched adults had been on the rise for three years, leaving one out of three adults unchurched.[3] Nevertheless, there is more openness to spiritual answers today than in previous decades. Two-thirds of unchurched adults want to experience God in a deeper and more tangible and significant way.[4] But Americans are not automatically turning to the church for this experience, as did their grandfathers and grandmothers. Instead they are trying counterfeit spiritual remedies.

THE SUPPLY

If you know the God of the Bible, you certainly know there is no problem on the supply side of the spiritual economics equation. "Now to him who is able to do immeasurably more than all we ask or imagine," wrote the apostle Paul (Ephesians 3:20–21), "according to his power that is at work within us, to him be glory in the church and in Christ Jesus throughout all generations, for ever and ever! Amen."

God's resources are limitless; his grace and love have no boundaries. And he longs to pour out this spiritual wealth on desperate and spiritually needy people. Paul wrote to the Christians in Philippi, "And my God will meet all your needs according to his glorious riches in Christ Jesus" (Philippians 4:19).

Given that we worship a God of *unlimited abundance*, the spiritual problem is clearly *not* a matter of supply. This leaves only one alternative: distribution. Simply put, the ways in which we've been delivering the spiritual goods have not been working. The idea, for example, that we can open a "distribution center" on some street corner and expect those in spiritual need to come to us has not worked. In fact, God did not intend for it to work. God is not in the retail business. He has chosen one-on-one mass distribution as his method to distribute his grace.

GOD'S DISTRIBUTION METHOD

It's fascinating to consider that, of all the methods the Creator of the universe could have used to spread his grace to the world, he chose to use men and women—ordinary Christians—not a few select, elite spokespersons. As he departed this earth, Jesus told his followers, "And you will be my witnesses in Jerusalem, and in all Judea and Samaria, and to the ends of the earth" (Acts 1:8).

God calls you and me as his witnesses, and we do not need to search hard to find a mission field. Our mission field is the place where we already spend most of our time, namely, our workplace. By being an ambassador for Jesus in the workplace, each of us can become a pipeline of God's grace to people who would never darken the doorway of a church. Now *that* is distribution!

God wants to use us to accomplish something so grand we can hardly imagine its significance. For each person this *something to be accomplished* is totally unique. Sound daunting? Relax! God has given you everything you need.

EVANGELISM AS A PROCESS

Many Christians of our generation were taught mechanical, aggressive (some would say intrusive) methods of evangelism that produced minimal results, despite the claims made by the organizations espousing these methods. I (Bill), motivated partly by guilt, took part in several evangelism seminars or courses, but the results became predictable. I would get inspired, go out and try what I'd learned, fail, stop trying—and feel even more guilty. I finally concluded that I just wasn't gifted to share my faith with others, which made me feel like a substandard Christian.

> The longer I am in business, the more passionate I become to be the hands, the feet extended of Christ. I see so many people who have not known God, don't think about God, don't talk about God. I want to provoke people to at least think about God. I want them to experience the love of Christ through me.
>
> *Anne Beiler, food service*

In the medical arena, I (Walt) found that an aggressive approach to evangelism was not only uncomfortable (both for me and my patients) but was also largely unfruitful. One day I just quit trying, content to consider my practice as merely a secular "tentmaking" operation while carrying on my ministry in the context of church life. Yet my heart was troubled. Every day I saw twenty to thirty non-Christian patients who desperately needed both physical and spiritual healing, and I came to believe I had nothing to offer them in the latter area.

The problem was that, as with many Christians, we (both authors) thought of evangelism as an *event*—a point in time when we mechanically recite the facts of the gospel message and encourage non-Christians to place their faith in Jesus. It was liberating for each of us to discover that evangelism, according to the Bible, is not an event but a *process*. Evangelism is organic—a lot more like farming than selling. This concept radically changed our lives and our ministries—Walt's in medicine and Bill's in professional ministry.

Event-centered evangelism defines success as getting a person to pray to receive Jesus as personal Savior. But when evangelism is seen as an organic process, this "decision" is only the climactic step of a long process that God uses to draw a person to himself. God's process typically enlists a number of people with a variety of gifts—each playing a different but vital role in helping someone take a step closer to Jesus. Accepting God's gift of salvation—obviously the goal of evangelism—is dependent on many steps before it. Bill Kraftson of Search Ministries observes that each Christian who encounters a non-Christian is like a link in a chain. "It's great to be the last link in the chain," says Kraftson, "but it's not more important than any other link. We just need to make sure we're not the missing link." Jim Petersen of the Navigators likewise views conversion as a process: "Few of us make it in one big decision. Instead, it's a multitude of small choices—mini-decisions that a person makes toward Jesus."[5]

THE DISTRIBUTION PROCESS

The Bible consistently employs an organic rather than a mechanical model to explain how God draws a person to himself. Paul uses the agrarian analogy in his passionate comments about the growing factions competing in the Corinthian church:

> What, after all, is Apollos? And what is Paul? Only servants, through whom you came to believe—as the Lord has assigned to each his task. I planted the seed, Apollos watered it, but God made it grow. So neither he who plants nor he who waters is anything, but

only God, who makes things grow. The man who plants and the man who waters have one purpose, and each will be rewarded according to his own labor. For we are God's fellow workers; you are God's field, God's building.

1 Corinthians 3:5–9

After speaking with the Samaritan woman at the well, Jesus uses the organic model to teach his disciples about the process of evangelism. The disciples were about to lead people to Jesus—or as he puts it, "reap" in a field that had previously been cultivated and planted by others:

Do you not say, "Four months more and then the harvest"? I tell you, open your eyes and look at the fields! They are ripe for harvest. Even now the reaper draws his wages, even now he harvests the crop for eternal life, so that the sower and the reaper may be glad together. Thus the saying "One sows and another reaps" is true. I sent you to reap what you have not worked for. Others have done the hard work, and you have reaped the benefits of their labor.

John 4:35–38

Jesus also uses an agrarian analogy to explain why some people respond to the word of God while others don't:

A farmer went out to sow his seed. As he was scattering the seed, some fell along the path, and the birds came and ate it up. Some fell on rocky places, where it did not have much soil. It sprang up quickly, because the soil was shallow. But when the sun came up, the plants were scorched, and they withered because they had no root. Other seed fell among thorns, which grew up and choked the plants. Still other seed fell on good soil, where it produced a crop—a hundred, sixty or thirty times what was sown.

Matthew 13:3–8

The seed—"the message about the kingdom" (Matthew 13:19)—falls on soils at varying stages of cultivation, representing the varying degrees of readiness of the human heart. The path—representing hard, uncultivated hearts—can't receive God's word. The rocky places and thorny soils—partially cultivated hearts—receive the words, but life can't flourish. The good soil—well-cultivated hearts—brings forth an abundant harvest.

Jesus' point is clear: A person's journey toward a relationship with him and the experience of eternal life is a process—a long process. And as with raising a crop, a lot of hard work is required before there is any talk of harvesting.

JESUS' GUIDE TO ORGANIC EVANGELISM

Based on an agrarian model, evangelism can be divided into four phases: cultivating, planting, harvesting, and multiplying. According to Jesus, the hard work of evangelism is not the harvest phase but the cultivation phase. Cultivation focuses on the soil of the human heart, which includes addressing emotional barriers. It requires our presence with non-Christians. The goal of cultivation is to help others begin to see the benefits of being a child of God. An important part of cultivation is to develop trust in the messenger, for if people don't trust us, they will never trust our message. Thus, the first step entails building relationships and then living in a way that creates trust. This does not mean we must live impeccable lives, which is something that can't be done anyway. But we can live authentically and honestly— demonstrating to others that we ourselves are in need of grace.

The planting phase addresses intellectual barriers—misconceptions, misinformation, and ignorance about God and the Christian faith. It requires thoughtful conversation as part of planting seeds of biblical truth, seeds designed to build an understanding of who Jesus is, what he wants from us, and what he wants to do for us. As we develop relationships with non-Christians and they become attracted to what Jesus is doing in us, we can begin to explain how Jesus has made, and continues to make, a difference in our lives. It begins slowly, with just enough truth to pique interest. As curiosity grows, so does the appetite for the truth. As non-Christians come to grips with spiritual truth, they are likely to discover significant discrepancies between the Bible and their way of thinking or philosophy of life. They'll need answers—presented patiently and humbly—to their intellectual questions.

MICRODECISIONS OF FAITH[6]

DISCIPLE	Chooses to live by faith	+5	**MULTIPLYING**	SPEAKS TO THE WHOLE PERSON ADDRESSES: SOCIAL BARRIERS TO OVERCOME: ISOLATION BY: PARTICIPATION IN THE BODY GOAL: GROWTH ANSWERS: WILL I LIVE FOR CHRIST? EXAMPLES: JERUSALEM CHURCH (ACTS 2:41–47) THE CHURCH AT ANTIOCH (ACTS 11:19–26)
	Chooses to share faith	+4		
	Makes Christlike choices	+3		
BELIEVER	Joins in community life	+2		
	Assimilates God's Word	+1		
	Trusts in Christ	0	**HARVESTING**	SPEAKS TO: THE WILL ADDRESSES: VOCATIONAL BARRIERS TO OVERCOME: INDECISION AND UNWILLINGNESS TO CHANGE BY: PRAYER & PERSUASION GOAL: TRUE CHRIST ANSWERS: WILL I TRUST CHRIST? EXAMPLES: PAUL BEFORE AGRIPPA (ACTS 26:1–29)
SEEKER	Turns from self-trust	-1		
	Sees Christ as the answer	-2		
	Recognizes spiritual need	-3		
SPECTATOR	Considers the truth of the gospel	-4	**PLANTING**	SPEAKS TO: THE MIND ADDRESSES: INTELLECTUAL BARRIERS TO OVERCOME: IGNORANCE, MISCONCEPTIONS & ERROR BY: PRESENTATION GOAL: UNDERSTANDING ANSWERS: WHO IS JESUS? WHAT DOES HE WANT FROM ME? EXAMPLES: ETHIOPIAN EUNUCH (ACTS 8:26–39)
	Understands the implications	-5		
	Aware of the gospel	-6		
	Recognizes relevance of the Bible	-7		
SKEPTIC	Looks positively at the Bible	-8	**CULTIVATING**	SPEAKS TO: THE EMOTIONS ADDRESSES: EMOTIONAL BARRIERS TO OVERCOME: DENIAL, INDIFFERENCE, FEAR & ANTAGONISM BY: YOUR PRESENCE GOAL: ATTRACTION, TRUST YOU ANSWERS: WHAT'S IN IT FOR ME? EXAMPLES: WOMAN AT THE WELL (JOHN 4:4–30) NICODEMUS (JOHN 3:1–21) MATTHEW 13:1–23
	Recognizes difference in the messenger	-9		
	Aware of the messenger	-10		
CYNIC	Going his/her own way	-11		
	Avoids the truth	-12		

The *harvesting* phase focuses on a person's will and its resistance to make a decision to trust Jesus. Even after someone's emotional and intellectual barriers have been broken down, the will remains. Men and women can neither think nor feel their way into God's kingdom. Though these elements are foundational, ultimately every human being must make a choice. Involvement during this phase requires prayer and continued conversation toward the goal of the person's receiving Jesus as Savior. In harvesting, we graciously persuade and consistently pray for God to draw our friend to himself.

The final phase, *multiplying*, entails implanting the new life into a community where it can grow and flourish. The goals of this phase are growth and reproduction. When new life is birthed, we need to give it proper care, ensuring that it has an environment that encourages growth and development toward maturity.

What's Right for Your Workplace?

If our efforts to share our faith publicly are to bear fruit, they must take into account contemporary cultural attitudes as well as realities in the twenty-first-century workplace. People are under pressure; schedules are tight. Each working environment is distinctive; relationships between and among supervisors and subordinates, or between employees and clients or patients, vary. A cookie-cutter approach to evangelism is doomed. In fact, some of the old gospel-sharing methods are unwise, if not flat-out unethical. A workable model for evangelism must respect the nonbeliever's integrity and vulnerability while also considering the professional's fiduciary responsibility.

> As a younger Christian, I was much more aggressive about sharing my faith. Now I am much more aware that it is God's work. I am just trying to be faithful on a day-to-day basis. I am much more cautious, because the battle is severe, and if it ever becomes known organizationally that you have an agenda, you can get in trouble.
>
> *Jack Alexander,*
> *travel and hospitality industry*

We have found that when people who are not gifted evangelists overemphasize the harvesting phase, they produce more frustration than fruit. They may even further harden the soil of unbelieving hearts. However, when these same men and women exercise their God-given gifts in the cultivating phase of evangelism, they have many more planting and harvesting opportunities. Evangelism is organic. Although this may come as a surprise to some, it is no surprise to any farmer—or to God.

All of us who follow Jesus must think carefully about how we can best make him known in our own workplace, given its particular limitations and constraints. Some work environments afford greater freedom and flexibility to spend time talking about spiritual topics. Others (such as a doctor's office) are highly scheduled and restrictive, allowing virtually no time for prolonged conversations. Some work environments are even hostile with regard to spiritual talk. Those who have a fiduciary responsibility and hold a professional knowledge unavailable to those they serve must take great care not to exploit another's position or situation. Whatever your arena, and however aggressive your workplace may allow you to be, being a "religious jerk" is never appropriate!

Throughout history and today we have witnessed various models for evangelism. We have identified five.

The *proclamational evangelism* model features public preaching and announcing the truth to a large audience. The best-known proclamational evangelist of our time is Billy Graham. Proclamation is modeled in the New Testament by John the Baptist, Jesus, Peter, Stephen, and Paul—all of whom preached the gospel to audiences.

Confrontational evangelism occurs when someone initiates a conversation with an individual (usually a stranger) with the specific aim of leading the person to Jesus. The Bible includes a few examples of this kind of evangelism: Jesus with Nicodemus, Jesus with the Samaritan woman, and Philip with the Ethiopian eunuch. Campus Crusade for Christ popularized this model. In the 1960s and 1970s, when the great search for truth was on at the university campus, this method fit the culture perfectly and was instrumental in both Bill's and Walt's journey of faith and understanding of the gospel.

Though many people are intimidated by talking to people they've never met, there are Christians who love to talk to perfect strangers about Jesus. They come back from business trips with incredible stories about how they met this or that stranger and led him or her in a dramatic way to Jesus. It's easy to think of these individuals as the gifted evangelists who are set apart to carry out the bulk of evangelistic activity for God.

While some people may be ready to hear about Jesus, not as many people are as ready to hear about Jesus from a perfect stranger as they once were. While making the gospel clear, the danger of confrontation is twofold. First, if a person feels pressure to respond before he or she is ready, the experience can create another emotional barrier that must be overcome before the person will trust Jesus. Second, when people who are not gifted evangelists force themselves into this mold, the result is rarely a positive experience—for the evangelist or the evangelized.

Intentional evangelism refers to creating opportunities to expose friends and colleagues to Jesus in a nonreligious, nonthreatening atmosphere. It's what Matthew (also known as Levi) did when he became a follower of Jesus. Instead of inviting his disreputable friends to the synagogue, he asked them to his home for dinner (see Luke 5:27–29).

In the intentional evangelism model, someone hosts a nonthreatening event that creates in non-Christian friends a sense of curiosity, which the host can intentionally pursue after the event. The event is more about sparking an interest than making converts. Intentional evangelism is based on forming a relationship of significant trust with a non-Christian friend and on the hope that the event will stimulate the non-Christian without causing him or her to feel "set up." This usually means that the event will not feature a pushy appeal to trust Jesus.

Events might feature a speaker that non-Christians would be interested in hearing. For several years I (Bill) hosted what we called the Leadership Breakfast during the pro-am golf tournament in Tyler, Texas. Several of the touring pros from the PGA are believers. Each year we invited one of them to talk a little about golf and to tell his faith story. Christians were encouraged to host a table and invite friends. More than three hundred men and women, many of whom wouldn't dream of attending church, came to hear a professional golfer. Another type of intentional evangelistic event is a forum, or discussion party. Rather than focusing on a speaker, this gathering is centered around discussion of questions people have about God or Christianity. Search Ministries and the Alpha course are two examples.

Passive evangelism uses symbols, objects, or art to arouse curiosity in the observer. We sometimes call this "trotline evangelism," after the fishing practice of baiting a series of hooks on a line, then leaving and coming back later to check the line. You put out the bait and hope a fish — or, in the case of evangelism, a person — bites. Religious art on the wall, tracts and magazines left in offices and waiting rooms, even Bibles, are conspicuously placed in hopes that someone may ask a question about God. The Old Testament is full of symbols designed to create curiosity, and many aspects of the Jewish ceremonial law were designed to draw people toward asking questions. Even the temple in Jerusalem was, in some sense, a giant symbolic tract designed to teach people how to approach God.

The benefit of this model is that it's always at work, even when you're not. It continues to say something even while you are absent or silent. The drawback is that it lacks subtlety. What's more, if the office atmosphere doesn't match the decor, a credibility problem arises. If you announce by what you put on the walls that you are a follower of Jesus, you'd better be sure to reflect the values of Jesus in the way you speak and act.

Relational evangelism builds a bridge of friendship based on common ground between a Christian and non-Christian. Relational evangelists see evangelism as a process rather than an event. In this model, success is measured on the basis of helping a person take one more step toward Jesus today.

This type of evangelism was the backbone of the strategy that resulted in the growth of the early church from a few hundred on the day of Pentecost to over half a million by the end of the first century. Christians everywhere chatted about Jesus to their friends, relatives, work associates, customers, masters, slaves, and fellow soldiers. According to church growth experts Win and Charles Arn, "Webs of *common kinship* (the larger family), *common friendship* (friends and neighbors), and *common associates* (work associates and people with common interests or recreational pursuits) are still the paths most people follow in becoming Christians today."[7]

The Arns cite the results of a survey in which approximately 14,000 people were asked the question, "What or who was responsible for your coming to Christ and your church?"[8] Eight responses were rated as follows:

1. A "special need" drew them	1–2 percent
2. They just "walked in"	2–3 percent
3. A pastor	5–6 percent
4. Church "visitation"	1–2 percent
5. Sunday school	4–5 percent
6. Evangelistic crusade or television show	0.5 percent
7. A church "program"	2–3 percent
8. A "friend/relative"	75–90 percent

The results of this survey highlight the importance of forming solid relationships (friendships) as part of the process of evangelism, regardless of which of the above models of evangelism you may employ.

This book explores the specifics of how to engage actively and fruitfully in the evangelistic task. The *fact* that we ought to be engaged in this task should not be an issue. After all, another person's eternal destiny is at stake: Revelation 20:15 declares, "If anyone's name was not found written in the book of life, he was thrown into the lake of fire."

The decision to go public with our faith affects believers as well. To refuse to join God as a distribution point of his grace is an act of blatant disregard for God's will and plan for our lives. We cannot stop the flow of grace without doing harm to ourselves. Paul singles out the sharing of our faith as a key to our mature spiritual identity: "I pray that you may be active in sharing your faith, so that you will have a full understanding of every good thing we have in Christ" (Philemon 6).

Certain functions are essential for human life—breathing, drinking, and eating being among them. These functions keep us alive and growing. If we want to remain spiritually alive and growing, we *must* speak of our faith with others. It's a sustaining requirement of spiritual life.

We are all workers in the Father's field. When we express our faith at our workplace, we join in his process of drawing men and women to himself. For most of us, it won't involve preaching to groups or aggressively talking to strangers about their relationship with Jesus. Instead, it will focus on the *cultivating* phase, doing what Jesus called "the hard work" (John 4:38)—building meaningful relationships with people over time.

THE BOTTOM LINE

Evangelism is not an event but a relational process, and God has gifted each of us to play a critical role in drawing men and women to himself.

Called to the Workplace

Chris would have been the last person to call himself an evangelist. He reluctantly signed up for a short-term mission trip to Cuba and came home full of stories of how he had seen God at work as the team went from house to house sharing the gospel. His new enthusiasm for declaring his faith was both heartwarming and a bit surprising.

After returning from Cuba, however, he felt increasingly dissatisfied with his marketing work at a large firm. He struggled with the feeling that to continue in his profession was somehow to choose God's second best for his life. *Perhaps I should quit my job to attend seminary,* he thought. He shared this "crazy idea" with his best friend, who told Chris to keep his job and use his vacation time to "do ministry."

But it seemed to Chris a colossal waste of time to spend most of his year working so that he could spend a couple of weeks doing what was truly important. *How can I waste so much time at a regular job,* he thought, *when so many people are facing an eternity without God?*

Chris began taking classes at a local seminary, but he lasted only about eighteen months. It wasn't the spiritual utopia he had anticipated. He later told me (Bill), "I guess seminary wasn't what God had planned for me." Chris returned to his "regular job," his enthusiasm for his faith floundering.

Unfortunately, Chris never considered his workplace as a mission field for sharing his faith in the way he longed to. In fact, when asked about allowing his passion to influence people's lives at his workplace, Chris thought the idea was inappropriate—and people there weren't interested anyway.

Chris is far from alone. We've talked to thousands of Christians who are frustrated by their inability to make a difference for God in their workplace. On Sunday morning, after the parting blessing is pronounced, they walk out of church into real life, seeing little or no connection between the worlds of faith and work. The six days between Sundays seem to them like a spiritual black hole.

THE SACREDNESS OF THE SECULAR

The average Christian sees a distinct difference between his or her work and the work of the local pastor. This view is rooted in a worldview that consists of two contrasting realities. "God's world" values activities such as prayer, Bible study, worship, meditation, and evangelism—in other words, "spiritual activities." In contrast, the so-called "real world" values work, finance, politics, pop music, the Internet, Monday night football, and the stock market. This "real world" worships at the altar of *power*, *prestige*, and *position*.

A few years ago I (Bill) attended a large gathering where the speaker honored the pastors in the audience by calling them forward for a blessing, proclaiming that they had the "highest calling" from God. The crowd affirmed this misconception—that these were God's real heroes. After the event, I talked to several people, and not one of them challenged the teaching that vocational Christian work is in essence the only work that really matters in the kingdom of God.

By no means do we wish to diminish the value of those who are called to careers in professional ministry. (In fact, at the time of this writing, both authors are working full-time with Christian ministries.) But let us keep in mind that at least three-fourths of the men and women from the Bible whom we call "heroes" were not in full-time ministry. They "wasted their time" working in "secular" jobs. Consider Abraham, for example, the father of the Jewish nation. He was not a professional priest but a rancher who followed God west and built a livestock empire on the open range. The patriarch Joseph started out on the family ranch but was abducted and taken to a foreign country where he rose to a top governmental position and saved the Near East from famine by his savvy grain futures trading.

Daniel is known as a prophet, but professionally he was chief adviser to several kings—a government worker who was employed well into his eighties. David became a professional soldier and later the ruler of his country. Nehemiah was a career bureaucrat who became the general contractor over a large government rehabilitation project. Even the ideal woman of Proverbs 31 receives accolades for executing several entrepreneurial ventures in real estate and textiles while practicing her other profession of being a family manager.

Did all these individuals miss God's best by *wasting time* in so-called "secular" pursuits? If so, we should also conclude that Jesus spent close to 90 percent of his earthly life wasting his time wielding a saw, hammer, and chisel. If God the Son planned to spend only thirty-plus years on earth, why did he "waste" 90 percent of it in secular work?

As a young man Tom started a business in Southern California that grew into a successful enterprise. Tom's competence and character meshed—resulting in an

> I had said to the Lord, "If you bless us and provide for us, someday I would like to do some mission work." Little did I know that it wasn't going to be in Nigeria or Afghanistan but right here in Holland, Michigan, with this new company. We committed this business to the Lord and asked for guidance and direction; twelve years later we are having a wonderful time, and we are touching and changing lives.
>
> *Jack DeWitt,*
> *frozen foods*

outstanding reputation in his community. He was overjoyed to see how God used his testimony and his company. Over several years, he saw several of his employees and customers begin a personal relationship with God and grow in their faith.

Over breakfast one morning, Tom's pastor inquired, "Tom, have you ever considered *really* giving your life to God—working full-time for the Lord?"

Tom felt confused. "Pastor," he explained, almost hesitantly, "I feel that what I'm doing now *is* a form of full-time work for the Lord."

The pastor smiled. "Tom, there's no doubt that God has used you in amazing ways. But the work you're in is secular. I think God is calling you to consider becoming involved in something higher."

Over the months, the two men talked more. Eventually, Tom sold his business and accepted an administrative role in a mission organization. He was in that role when I (Walt) met him at the time he became my patient. He had been with the organization about two years and was displaying an array of physical symptoms. As I got to know Tom and studied the results of medical tests, I became convinced that he was suffering from anxiety and depression.

The symptoms responded well to medications, but the medications didn't begin to touch the root of the problem. One day I asked, "Tom, do you think you're doing what God wants you to do?"

His eyes teared up as he gazed out the window. "Walt, I think God had me right where he wanted me — in my business in California." He paused and continued, "Do you think there's a difference between sacred work and secular work?"

"I don't think so," I responded. "I think the real difference is between sacred and secular people." I continued, "Tom, if you and your pastor go to work for different reasons, at least one of you is going to work for the wrong reason." Tom frowned as he absorbed the implication of this statement.

THE ROOTS OF THE FAULTY THINKING

The mistaken conception that some men and women do sacred work for God while the rest of humanity settles for less than God's best by doing secular work is an ancient one, but it has no basis in Scripture. In Western thought, this idea developed from Greek philosophy, which taught that any kind of menial work with physical materials was beneath the gods or men who had the means to choose how they spent their time. Slaves did the menial work, while those with means opted to spend their time in pursuits of the mind — religion or philosophy. This worldview was crystallized in the heresy of Gnosticism, which divided reality into two parts — the material realm (entirely evil) and the spiritual realm (entirely good).

Confucius, father of much of Eastern philosophy, taught virtually the same thing. Whether from East or West, most religions view the physical world as base, in some way unclean and beneath the dignity of the truly pious. This viewpoint has come to dominate the way many religious people worldwide think of spiritual priorities.

This mistaken notion has plagued the church from the very beginning, with the result that "worldly activities" are viewed as a major distraction to a person's spiritual development. No wonder Chris and Tom and so many others are confused about what it really means to follow Jesus day after day.

THE IMPACT OF FAULTY THINKING

The dichotomous worldview that artificially separates the sacred from the secular has had a disastrous impact on Christians in the workplace and even on the church's vision for ministry. British writer and Christian apologist Dorothy Sayers (1893-1957) wrote:

> In nothing has the church so lost her hold on reality as in her failure to understand and respect the secular vocation. She has allowed work and religion to become separate departments, and is astonished to find that, as a result, the secular work of the world is turned to purely selfish and destructive ends, and that the greater part of the world's intelligent workers have become irreligious, or at least, uninterested in religion.[1]

THE IMPACT ON INDIVIDUAL CHRISTIANS

Accepting the secular-sacred split invariably leads Christians in the workplace to feel caught between the demands of two worlds. On the one hand, you sense the need to engage in work, to be a responsible citizen, and to provide for the physical needs of life. On the other hand, you hear the voice of this faulty worldview telling you that you're wasting your time in your work and that you should spend more time pursuing God through spiritual activities. It is difficult, if not impossible, to live successfully if you allow these forces to tug at your heart. There will be certain consequences to pay.

Abandoned Advantages

One of the consequences is the failure to recognize the resources you have working on your behalf. Imagine for a moment that you've been given the following opportunities:

- Consult with Jack Welch (former CEO of General Electric) on an important business decision.
- Have Bill Gates (founder of Microsoft and one of the wealthiest men in the world) as your financial backer and consultant during a crucial financial decision.
- Talk with Richard Bolles (author of What Color Is Your Parachute?) about the pros and cons of the new job opportunity you've just been offered.

And what if these men not only made themselves available to you but also were sincerely interested in your success at work? What if they were waiting for you daily at your office or job site, ready to walk with you through every decision, crisis, and success? You'd be a fool to ignore their offers of support. Yet this is exactly what many Christians do every day when they ignore God's interest and presence in their workplace.

Listen to this reassuring promise in the context of the kind of work environment we have today: "Keep your lives free from the love of money and be content with what you have, because God has said, 'Never will I leave you; never will I forsake you.' So we say with confidence, 'The Lord is my helper; I will not be afraid. What can man do to me?'" (Hebrews 13:5–6). Imagine making a decision about a convoluted issue, firm in the conviction that what God promised is true: "I will lead the blind by ways they have not known, along unfamiliar paths I will guide them" (Isaiah 42:16).

Lack of Spiritual Motivation

If the highlight of your spiritual life is going to church once a week, dropping some money in the offering plate, and not giving the preacher too much trouble—or if you think you've fulfilled the bulk of your spiritual responsibility by warming a pew on Sunday morning—then just how spiritual do you need to be? Not very!

If I'm on the reserve team, do you think I'm going to be passionately disciplined about being in shape? Probably not. If the *real* players on the spiritual field are the religious professionals, then ordinary Christians can leave the heavy lifting to them. Why sacrifice some sleep by getting up early to spend time focusing on my relationship with God if he really isn't interested in what I'm doing until next Sunday? The fact is, few of us will ever feel personally responsible enough to deepen our faith and learn to articulate it well *unless* we think it will really make a difference.

Moral Compromise

Unfortunately, some Christians don't look much different from their non-Christian coworkers. They talk the same, have the same work habits, compromise on the same issues, and entertain themselves in the same ways as those who have never met God personally. In some cases, the only difference between Christians and non-Christians is where they spend an hour or so on Sunday morning.

Marginalized Faith

The question begs to be asked: How can we be serious about God if we devote the largest measure of our time, talent, treasure, and energy to a part of life we think God has no interest in? Dorothy Sayers asked the question this way: "How can anyone remain interested in a religion which seems to have no concern with nine-tenths of his life?"[2]

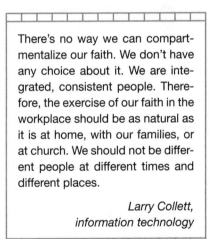

There's no way we can compartmentalize our faith. We don't have any choice about it. We are integrated, consistent people. Therefore, the exercise of our faith in the workplace should be as natural as it is at home, with our families, or at church. We should not be different people at different times and different places.

Larry Collett,
information technology

If you are living with a divided secular-sacred worldview, then you'll tend to make one of two choices: You will separate yourself as much as possible from worldly things, or you will forget God and devote yourself to the pursuit of success as the world defines it. Trying to live in both worlds is schizophrenic, dishonest, and profoundly crippling. Chances are neither your work nor your faith will be very satisfying.

THE IMPACT ON THE WORKPLACE

This dichotomous secular-sacred worldview has had a pronounced impact on the workplace. I (Walt) remember a conversation I had with a woman named Shelley. Her husband worked for a large international ministry. When their kids were grown, Shelley reentered the profession she had left to raise her family. One day I asked her about the differences in the business world since she left it over two decades earlier.

She thought for a moment. "I'm not surprised at the faster pace and the increasing importance of technology. But what really blows me away is the noticeable loss of care and service. The whole business world seems to be *all about me*. The only reason people seem to care about someone else is for what that person can do to help them reach their goals. It's really a dog-eat-dog world now." Shelly paused. "I'm thinking of getting out. I may try to get a position at the ministry."

This woman, whose godly influence the business world desperately needs, is considering withdrawing into the "holy huddle."

Eroded Ethical Foundations

It shouldn't surprise us, given the abandonment of the workplace by the church, that godless thinking and misguided values have come to dominate the workplace. If you want to be a success today, it's likely that your workplace—not the Bible—determines your value system. The corporate scandals in 2002 will provide ethical case studies for years. Dishonesty and greed defined the values of corporate officers, boards, and auditors of a number of massive corporations, leading to "cooked books" that vastly inflated company earnings. When these deceitful practices were uncovered, the loss of trust in the market as a whole was disastrous.

To say it's all about money is to be overly simplistic. It's really about what money buys. Three elements are deemed by many as absolutely essential in today's workplace:

- power—How many people report to you and obey your orders?
- prestige—Who looks up to you and envies your position?

- possessions—Where do you live, where do you go on vacation, what do you drive?

Lying, cheating, and stealing won't necessarily disqualify you from staying in the game, but failing to have power, position, and possessions will.

Lost Personal Trust

Hang around the workplace awhile and you're bound to hear someone say, "It's not personal. It's business." This phrase is the practical equivalent of a permission slip to do harm to someone. The fact is, business *is* personal. Without people, business doesn't exist. Can you imagine someone saying, "Nothing personal. It's the Lord's work"? Somehow we know that God's work is very personal. He cares about people. But declare your independence from God, and "anything you can get away with" is going to be your mode of operation.

Questions such as "Is it legal?" and "Will it make money?" have too often replaced the question "Is it the right thing to do?" No wonder trust has become a depleted commodity. How can any market be truly productive without people who trust each other making a commitment to work together? But how can they trust each other when their own selfish interest is what they value most?

THE IMPACT ON THE CHURCH

The secular-sacred divide has not just invaded the workplace but also the church. A few years ago, a church near my (Walt's) home called a new pastor. The former pastor had taught and equipped, but the men and women in the pew were the ministers—and their impact on the community was notable. The new pastor's views of church growth met with approval, and he slowly transformed the church essentially into a staff-led business. More and more people attended worship, and the budget grew tenfold in five years; however, the impact on the community began declining, and the men and women who had once been the most active in ministry quietly left for churches that needed and desired their giftedness.

Don't misunderstand us. We're not saying that Church Street can't learn from Wall Street. We can—a lot! But when power, prestige, and possessions—as opposed to biblical teachings that value glorifying God, serving others, and receiving eternal rewards—become the measuring sticks of success, we've got problems.

Undermined Godly Motives

Worldly values and philosophies have crept in and gained access to the pulpit. In the minds of many pastors today, the size of one's membership and budget has for all intents and purposes become *the* criteria for a successful ministry. More energy seems to be expended on marketing principles than on prayer and other spiritual disciplines.

You may be thinking that now we are pledging allegiance to the secular-sacred distinction ourselves. Actually, we believe that good business principles are good for any organization—commercial or spiritual. We believe that God's work, whether done in the workplace or the worship place, should operate based on both prayer *and* sound business principles. But when the secular-sacred division is embraced, it becomes easy for contaminating influences to undermine godly motives. The truth is that it's usually easier to get the church out of the world than to get the world out of the church.

Misaligned Priorities

The church has also tended to improperly elevate spiritual matters above earthly matters, thereby marginalizing its impact on society. Too often, the church sees its most important day as Sunday. In actuality, Monday through Saturday are critical. The goal should not only be to get the community into the church but to get the church into the community, because in order to bring people to Jesus, we must bring Jesus to people.

On Monday morning, the church is not at the corner of Meadow and Central. It spreads out all over the community, the nation, and sometimes the world as men and women disperse to do their work. It's out there—on the street, in the classroom, at the workplace—where the kingdom of God meets the kingdom of this world. *That's* where the real battle is taking place.

Unprepared Workers

Mislocating the battle has led the church to a major tactical error. If the battle is *inside* the church, then the front-line duty can be assigned only to a few highly trained specialists. If the role of the nonprofessional is merely to provide support, there's little need to train and equip people in the pews for serious kingdom work. From the vantage point of the pew, if you don't see the need to be part of the kingdom, why take the risk?

When the church neglects to equip people to talk about their faith with friends, colleagues, and coworkers, it fails to make a genuine impact on the workplace and ends up marginalizing itself—a sad state of affairs, especially because people today are on the greatest soul search in human history.

WHAT DOES THE BIBLE TEACH?

The biblical worldview leaves no room for secular-sacred, dualistic thinking. Unlike the aloof gods of Greek or Eastern thought, the God of the Bible is actively involved in his world. He rolled up his sleeves, so to speak, as he engaged in creation. Note that the biblical words used to describe God's work of creation are physical and earthy:

> When the LORD God made the earth and the heavens ... the LORD God *formed* the man from the dust of the ground and *breathed into his nostrils* the breath of life, and the man became a living being.
>
> Now the LORD God had *planted* a garden in the east, in Eden; and there he put the man he had *formed.*
>
> Genesis 2:4b, 7–8, italics added

Interestingly, the Hebrew word used to describe God's work in creation is the same word often used to describe human labor: "By the seventh day God had finished the *work* he had been doing; so on the seventh day he rested from all his *work*" (Genesis 2:2, italics added). No wonder God has a high view of the physical world and the work we do in it. The author of Genesis writes, "God saw all that he had made, and it was very good" (Genesis 1:31).

Before there was ever a need for evangelism, God gave humans a commission he has yet to withdraw: "Be fruitful and increase in number; fill the earth and subdue it. Rule over the fish of the sea and the birds of the air and over every living creature that moves on the ground" (Genesis 1:28). When we go to our workplace to meet legitimate human needs, we are working for God—whether we realize it or not. Even though we may forget that God is in the workplace, he does not forget our work. Abraham Kuyper, nineteenth-century Dutch theologian and prime minister, said it well: "There is not one square inch of the entire creation about which Jesus Christ does not cry out, 'This is mine! This belongs to me!'"[3]

Several times in his letters, the apostle Paul reiterates God's claim over the workplace. The placement of these passages indicates that our work life is, in many ways, as important to God as our family life. Just as God is head of the family, he is also your boss at work:

> Slaves, obey your earthly masters in everything; and do it, not only when their eye is on you and to win their favor, but with sincerity of heart and reverence for the Lord. Whatever you do, work at it with all your heart, as working for the Lord, not for men, since you know that you will receive an inheritance from the Lord as a reward. It is the Lord Christ you are serving. Anyone who does wrong will be repaid for his wrong, and there is no favoritism.
>
> Masters, provide your slaves with what is right and fair, because you know that you also have a Master in heaven.
>
> Colossians 3:22–4:1

Though our circumstances today are different from the first century, the context is the same—the workplace. In Paul's day slaves comprised the bulk of the workforce in the Roman world. Rather than using the terms *employee* and *employer*, as he would if he were speaking to us today, he addressed slaves and masters.

Today, Paul would say something like this: At least three things that transcend time and circumstances have changed about your work if you are a follower of Jesus:

1. WE HAVE A NEW JOB DESCRIPTION

If we follow the job description given to the readers of Colossians, *we should go to work to serve others*—not to get others to serve us. We work not to gain power over others but to empower them. Whether I am an employee or an employer, a manager or the managed, the gospel truth expressed by Paul declares that I go to work not primarily for myself but for others. I must treat fairly the people I work for, giving them the work that is expected of me. I must treat fairly those who work for me, empowering them to do their work.

This is usually easier for those who are more people centered than task oriented or project directed. Nevertheless, God places us in particular situations so that we may both come to know him better and make him known to the people with whom we cross paths in the workplace. As we serve others in the workplace, we serve the Lord of the workplace.

Work is also an avenue to demonstrate excellence. Our work should always be done with integrity and excellence. "With sincerity" (Colossians 3:22) means literally "without wax." A common way to repair damage done in the kiln to a piece of pottery was to fill the cracks with wax, thus deceiving the purchaser. Paul exhorts us to be honest in all our actions—no wax in the cracks.

Whether someone is watching us or not, our work should be of the same quality—done out of pure motives, with nothing hidden. The truth is, we *are* always being watched, because Jesus, the Lord of the workplace, is always with us. Therefore, in everything we do, says Paul, we do it as though we are working for the Lord—as though he is physically watching and supervising us.

Paul also tells us that we must put our whole heart into our work. After all, the Lord of the workplace deserves it, but so do our colleagues and customers. Dorothy Sayers reminds us, "What the church should be telling him [an intelligent carpenter] is this: that the first demand that his religion makes on him is that he should make good tables."[4] Pursuing excellence in work is always the right thing to do. Just as we do, God recognizes good work when he sees it.

2. WE HAVE A NEW MOTIVE

Work is an avenue to demonstrate our love for God—a way for us to express our worship. I go to work not to gain personal prestige but to honor God. Paul indicates that work is a means of worship, of ascribing worth to God: "It is the Lord Christ you are serving" (Colossians 3:24).

Don't miss the shocking effect this must have had on Greek ears. It's hard to escape the idea that Paul sees all work as God's work: "*Whatever* you do, work at it with all your heart, as working for the Lord" (Colossians 3:23, italics added). *Whatever* includes a broad spectrum of activities, especially considering the fact that Paul is addressing slaves, some of whom did the most menial labor—things like emptying chamber pots. This word *whatever* strikes the death-blow to the idea that God's work and a person's daily work are separate. If you are meeting legitimate human needs, you are working for God.

Doing God's work in God's way allows you to fulfill the first commission given to humankind to "fill the earth and subdue it." The opening chapter of Genesis shows that God worked to create; and he created humanity in his image—as workers. Our working well and for his glory consists of acts of love and worship. (There are, of course, things we do that don't bring glory to God. If an activity is essentially sinful, no worthy motive can redeem it. Drug dealing, prostitution, or bank robbery will not be listed as a job in God's human resource department.)

> My work is worship to me. In that light, God puts me in contact with people who are divine appointments. Some of them are people I would call my business associates or employees, and others are called customers. In this massive amount of human interaction, I have an opportunity to embed a philosophy. The way we do business, the way we treat customers—eventually this gets embedded in the service provided.
>
> *Merrill Oster,*
> *business journalist*

Did you catch Paul's astounding claim that work is an essential part of the spiritual life? "Whatever you do," he writes, "work at it *with all your heart*" (Colossians 3:23, italics added). Any Christian who is comfortable with a secular-sacred dichotomy must explain how "work at it *with all your heart*" fits with Jesus' response to the expert of the law who asked him about the greatest commandment: "Love the Lord your God *with all your heart* and with all your soul and with all your mind" (Matthew 22:37, italics added). If doing your work is a separate department from loving God, then you must disobey one command in order to obey the other. On the other hand, if all work is God's work, then working heartily at something with the intention of bringing glory to God can be a supreme act of love for and worship of God.

3. WE HAVE A NEW SALARY STRUCTURE

Work is an avenue for eternal significance to the individual. We go to work not to get rich but to gain an eternal reward. Contrary to what some of us have heard from well-meaning individuals, as followers of Jesus our daily work now counts for eternity. The old adage "There are only two things of eternal significance—the Word of God and the souls of men" is just not valid—or biblical. Paul's statements here bring incredible dignity and eternal importance to even the most menial task.

KINGDOM BUSINESS IN THE WORKPLACE

When William Wilberforce made a serious commitment to follow Jesus, he went to John Newton, slave trader-turned-pastor (writer of the classic hymn "Amazing Grace") to discuss whether he should leave the British parliament and go to seminary. Newton wisely reminded Wilberforce, "Maybe God has you there for a purpose" — and indeed he did. As we'll discuss in our last chapter, Wilberforce became one of the strongest forces for Jesus in his generation.

When a spiritual mentor asked Danish attorney Valdemar Hvidt about his next challenge, Hvidt pointed to the biggest problem he could imagine in the 1930s—unemployment. With little prospect of success, Hvidt convened a group of associates who prayed for guidance. The ideas they implemented resulted in thousands of new jobs. When Nazi forces occupied the country in 1939 and Denmark faced

> You need to be aware of the opportunity and the responsibility you have to use your place of work as a mission field. Because you are aware of the opportunity, you can be opportunistic. If it is something in your consciousness, you are more apt to take advantage when those opportunities come along.
>
> *Jim Lindemann,*
> *manufacturing*

a darker problem than unemployment, Hvidt's prayer group became part of the Christian Resistance Movement.[5]

Please notice that neither Wilberforce nor Hvidt left the workplace in search of spiritual significance. They found it where God designed them to find it—*right where they were*. Although God may and surely does call some men and women to leave the workplace for professional ministry, it is the exception. He wants Christians to go to work for the same reason they go to church: to worship God and serve their fellow humans.

It stands to reason, then, that he expects us not only to serve him but also to enter into the joy of making him known in the workplace.

No matter how dominant secular-sacred thinking becomes, Jesus will never give up his claim on the world, including the workplace. He told his first-century followers—and us today—"I will build my church, and the gates of Hades will not overcome it" (Matthew 16:18). We believe that we will witness a new movement of God's Spirit in our time. We sense that men and women all over the world are realizing that their greatest influence and ministry may be right there in their workplace. No longer content to do the "pick-up work" of the kingdom, they are eager to be fully equipped to make a difference in their workplace.

THE BOTTOM LINE

You don't have to leave the workplace to know the joy of being used by God. He wants to use you right where you are.

3

IS ANYONE HUNGRY?

Toward the end of a long day, I (Bill) collapsed into the aisle seat of an airplane. I was tired, didn't want to talk to anyone, and hoped I wouldn't have to move until I arrived at my destination. Before long, however, an attractive young woman came down the aisle and said, "I'm in that window seat." We engaged in polite conversation as the flight took off. I discovered she was a successful backdrop artist in her late twenties, married, no kids. She stiffened when she found out I was a "religious professional." I, in turn, stereotyped her: a typical secular woman with no apparent spiritual interests and no sense of any need of God.

I had just addressed five hundred doctors about the importance of communicating their faith. Not more than two hours earlier I had made a point of saying that God has divine appointments for each Christian each day. I instructed the audience, "When you meet someone, ask yourself, 'What is God doing in this person's life, and what can I do to come alongside?'"

Although I'm not a gifted evangelist, it didn't take me long to realize that a quiet inner voice wasn't going to allow me to nap in peace. I opened my eyes. As we looked out at the sunset, I said casually, "Beautiful isn't it? God paints us a new picture every evening—no two alike. Now *that's* creativity!" I raised this "faith flag," not really expecting her to recognize it, much less salute it. But her response surprised me. For the next hour, like the woman at the well (John 4), she *pulled* the gospel out of me. She told me she was traveling home after breaking off an affair. She confessed that she felt guilty, hurt, and alone. In response, I told her what the Bible has to say about Jesus' ability to meet these very prevalent needs.

She wasn't ready to trust her life to a Stranger, but she was eager to learn more about him and the Bible. I still pray for her and ask

God to send other followers of Jesus into her life to help her take the next step toward a relationship with him. I was wrong about her lack of spiritual hunger. She was so famished that she was willing to spill her guts to a perfect stranger.

God reminded me of something important that day: America may be "one nation under God," but a lot of Americans are spiritually ignorant. This young woman raised in the Bible Belt had virtually no knowledge of the Bible for me to use as a conversational starting point. Even John 3:16 was new to her. But her biblical illiteracy didn't mean she was spiritually satisfied. This successful, together-looking woman was starving to death spiritually, and she knew it. She just had no clue that her only hope is Jesus and that the Bible has answers for her problems.

Sadly, she's not alone. As hostile and uninterested as some people may seem toward the Christianity they know about through the media, millions have a gnawing hunger. George Barna has uncovered this hunger in his research:

> Our surveys consistently detect a large (and growing) majority of adults who are dissatisfied and are searching for something more meaningful than bigger homes, faster paychecks, trimmer bodies, more erotic affairs, and extended leisure. Tens of millions of Americans are open to a set of spiritual truths that will set them free from the shackles of worldliness.[1]

That night on an airplane a hungry traveler had a divine appointment with a man who could share with her the food that would satisfy.

GET TO KNOW YOUR CUSTOMER

Here's an important question: If people are really hungry and I have food to offer, why aren't they buying? Marketing experts say that if you want someone to switch to your product or service, you need three things that will tip the scales in your favor (besides having a good product). As followers of Jesus who care about lost people, we can learn from these marketing principles.

1. What you offer customers must have an *overt benefit*. In other words, the customer needs to be able to see "what's in it for me." This benefit must be clearly communicated.
2. There must be a reason to believe that the claims made about the product or service are true. Your marketing must have *persuasive credibility*; it must be trustworthy. Both the claim(s) and the person making the claim(s) must be credible. Customers need to know why they should believe your claims.
3. The customer must be able to see a *dramatic difference* in his or her current situation and what *dramatic benefit* using your product or service will bring in comparison to anything else available on the market.

Whether you want people to believe that your company's product or service can change their lives or that Jesus can change their lives, it's critical to *know your customer*. Lest you think this sounds like a worldly perspective on evangelism, look at the market research Paul did in Athens:

> While Paul was waiting for them in Athens, he was greatly distressed to see that the city was full of idols. So he reasoned in the synagogue with the Jews and the God-fearing Greeks, as well as in the marketplace day by day with those who happened to be there. A group of Epicurean and Stoic philosophers began to dispute with him. Some of them asked, "What is this babbler trying to say?" Others remarked, "He seems to be advocating foreign gods." They said this because Paul was preaching the good news about Jesus and the resurrection. Then they took him and brought him to a meeting of the Areopagus, where they said to him, "May we know what this new teaching is that you are presenting?..."
>
> Paul then stood up in the meeting of the Areopagus and said: "Men of Athens, I see that in every way you are very religious. For as I walked around and *looked carefully* at your objects of worship, I even found an altar with this inscription: TO AN UNKNOWN GOD. Now what you worship as something unknown I am going to proclaim to you."
>
> Acts 17:16–19, 22–23, italics added

Notice that Paul didn't just blindly communicate in a vacuum. He learned what he could about his audience. He took time to understand the Athenians and their culture. Paul describes his "marketing philosophy" in his first letter to the Corinthians:

> Though I am free and belong to no man, I make myself a slave to everyone, to win as many as possible. To the Jews I became like a Jew, to win the Jews. To those under the law I became like one under the law (though I myself am not under the law), so as to win those under the law. To those not having the law I became like one not having the law (though I am not free from God's law but am under Christ's law), so as to win those not having the law. To the weak I became weak, to win the weak. I have become all things to all men so that by all possible means I might save some. I do all this for the sake of the gospel, that I may share in its blessings.
>
> 1 Corinthians 9:19–23

Obviously Paul wasn't talking about compromising moral standards for the sake of being accepted. He didn't change the content of his message, but he surely packaged it differently, tailoring it to the particular audience he was addressing at the time.

Who are you trying to influence? What do they like and dislike? What do they sense they need? What are they looking for (if anything) from God? What barriers must be overcome? What strategies are most effective today? What kind of person makes Jesus' message attractive to this audience? If, as George Barna suggests, half the people who don't follow Jesus say they are annoyed when people try to share their religious beliefs with them,[2] it could well be time to change the "marketing strategy."

THE MARKET REALITIES OF THE TWENTY-FIRST CENTURY

Connecting a consumer's need with a product or service calls for savvy market research. Just as every business must understand its customer, Christians need to understand the current market realities of sharing their faith. Unlike the late 1960s and early 1970s (the time when we (both authors) became Christians and were first trained to share our faith), we live in a day when men and women are no longer arguing the validity of Christianity (of course it's valid, they say, just as Hinduism, Islam, and Native American spiritism are valid). Their question is not validity but *relevance*. Interestingly, non-Christians rarely conclude that Christianity is not true. It's simply not applicable, they say, to life in the new millennium.

In addition, the picture of Christianity painted by a hostile media is anything but flattering. Usually painted in a rigid, unpleasant light, Christianity doesn't look like anything most people can relate to, much less experience.

Followers of Jesus who passionately want to tell others about the wonders of God's love have their work cut out for them. In many ways, we have less in common with those we work with than did believers in decades past. However, this is the time in history God has chosen for us to live. And no matter where we are on history's timeline, this principle holds true: The less we have in common with someone else, the more careful and thoughtful we must be when we communicate.

WE ARE A PLURALISTIC SOCIETY

For two hundred years, America was called "the great melting pot." Men and women came from all over the world to settle this land. As they came, they left the Old World behind to become Americans. They learned English, and their native languages were all but forgotten by the second generation. These folks were proud of their new identity and adopted new traditions.

The America of the twenty-first century is a very different world:

- 46.9 million Americans (17.9 percent) speak a language other than English in their homes.[3]
- Our foreign-born population has increased 191 percent from 1970 to 2000.[4]
- To obtain the data in the 2000 U.S. Census, the Census Bureau provided language assistance for forty-nine languages other than English.[5]

With the growing ethnic diversity has come religious diversity. Followers of other traditions, which we only read about in social studies when we were kids, now live next door. With ethnic and religious diversity has come a variety of worldviews that compete for recognition. No longer is the Judeo-Christian worldview the only force considered in determining values and understanding life.

But it's not only outside forces that have affected our culture. Philosophies once confined to the university have now largely become mainstreamed. Alternative views of sexuality, family, and life itself have made their way into the daily cultural debate.

If you go to work tomorrow, willing to tell others about the love and grace you've found in Jesus, to whom will you speak? The man in the office next to you may be a Pakistani—and probably a Muslim. The woman on the other side may be a radical feminist, perhaps a lesbian. The guy across the hall often brags of his womanizing. What do you say? How can you get your coworkers to listen to you long enough to tell them how much God loves them and longs to give them a satisfying life here on earth and a home in heaven when they die? If you don't take time to understand your audience, it's likely that doors will slam in your face.

Whether you see all this as a threat or as a privileged opportunity will in some way tell how much your worldview has been influenced either by culture or by the Bible. Do you believe that God loves these people and may want to use you to introduce them to him? What will they see in you that would cause them to be interested in what you believe?

WE ARE A BIBLICALLY IGNORANT CULTURE

At first glance, many people in our culture seem to be totally put off by religion. (This was my initial assessment of the woman I talked with on the plane.) But dig a little deeper, and you'll often discover that God is at work, preparing their hearts for your influence.

People are more interested in spiritual realities now than at any other period in our lifetime. However, for the first time in our country's history, a majority of people are looking for answers to their spiritual questions from sources other than the church and Christianity. To complicate matters, when broaching the subject of spirituality, we have a different beginning point than we did twenty-five years ago. People are biblically ignorant. We can no longer assume they know any of the biblical stories, characters, or principles on which we can then build a conversation. For example, seven out of ten adults have no clue what "John 3:16" means. Barely one-third of all adults (31 percent) know the meaning of the expression "the gospel." Nine out of ten American adults (86 percent) cannot accurately define the meaning of the "Great Commission."[6]

This is our reality, despite 320,000 churches, 800,000 ordained ministers, several networks devoted to religious broadcasting, evangelistic ministries that spend $200 million on television time and $100 million on radio broadcasts *each* year, 5,000 evangelistic parachurch organizations, and a Christian book and music industry that boasts $1 billion in annual revenues.[7] We're talking, but no one is listening—except maybe the choir.

Is it possible to make a spiritual impact on a secularized, egocentric culture that sees the church as irrelevant, boring, or negative? By all means! But not with a model that demands they come to a distribution center (read *church*) to receive God's grace from God's "official" spokesperson (read *pastor*). On Sunday mornings most non-Christians will more likely be "cocooning" at home or relaxing at the lake—not occupying a pew. Often these folks are not anti-God; they simply wonder, *Why bother? Why should I go back for another guilt trip on how much I should be doing for the church? I can't keep up with my schedule as it is! Why would I want to seek answers from leaders whose lives seem more screwed up than mine?*

But don't be misled. These individuals deeply feel their spiritual emptiness. Behind the clothes and cars that portray an "I've got it together!" look, there's a deep longing for meaning that is not being quenched by materialistic acquisitions.

Sadly, it will never occur to many people that Jesus has significant answers for their struggles unless someone *shows* them differently. The life of Jesus, not just the message, must present itself to them as lived out in a *seven-day-a-week faith*. Unless we show what Jesus is doing in our lives, non-Christians will miss what Jesus can do for them. Unless they see joy in us as we work, unless they see the peace Jesus gives us when we encounter difficult situations or ornery people, when we are disappointed or feel hurt or rejected, or when we get a bad diagnosis, they're not likely to get the message that Jesus can make a difference for them.

The strategy that compels them to come to a church building to receive the gospel from someone they don't know—someone who speaks what sounds like a foreign language—simply won't work. People will best be able to find Jesus when followers of Jesus bring Jesus to them, starting at their level of understanding and interest and accepting them where they are.

MODERNISM AND POSTMODERNISM[8]

Modernism	Postmodernism
Effects have causes	"Stuff happens"
"The Truth" is attainable	Nothing can be proven
Truth is discovered	"Truth" is constructed
Reason is trusted	Objective reason is denied
Values facts	Values relationships
Man is a biological machine	Man is a social being
Materialistic	Looking for meaning

WE ARE INCREASINGLY POSTMODERN IN OUTLOOK

The people you want to reach out to in your workplace, especially Americans born after 1960, are increasingly *postmodern* in outlook. The modern era began when rational, scientific thinking replaced during the Renaissance (fourteenth–seventeenth centuries) the superstitious thinking of the Dark Ages (about AD 500–1000). Although postmodernism is seen as a looming threat to the Christian faith, it is actually no more a threat than was modernism—just a different one. To help us understand, let's examine the two worldviews:

The modernist notion that effects have discoverable causes drove the scientific revolution. Postmodern America will likely see a decline in scientific pursuits because postmodernists believe that causes can't really be determined—or even if they could, it doesn't matter anyway.

The ramifications? Evidence for the existence of God that relies on cause-effect arguments is likely to have far less impact on people outside the scientific community than it has had in the past.

The Downside of Postmodernism

We see significant problems with the cultural shift toward postmodernism. Perhaps the most troublesome notion is the belief, or at least suspicion, that *everything is relative* — that there is no such thing as absolute truth and no clear line between right and wrong. This belief undermines the prospect for intelligent, rational dialogue on moral, ethical, and even factual issues.

If truth can't be discovered, and we're not sure of its relevance, why even bother to look for truth? Although the Bible is still respected by many as a book of wisdom, it's not unusual for people to consider it arrogant, unintelligent, and intolerant to believe that the Bible contains "the truth" any more than any other religious book does. Although we believe that reason as well as revelation can be used to rationally defend the superiority of a biblical value system, neither reason nor revelation carries much weight for a postmodernist.

If truth can't be discovered, a religious person's insistence that one can know right from wrong and can know the way to get to heaven is considered the height of arrogance and ignorance. Postmodernism has made some of its greatest inroads here. The deification of *tolerance* is tantamount to modernism's exaltation of reason. This cardinal virtue of postmodernism prejudices the mind against those of us who say we know the Truth. The common assumption is that we are intentionally deceiving others for the sake of our selfish agendas.

Experiences of deceit, dishonesty, and hypocrisy with our social, political, business, and religious leaders have led to deep distrust among the general public. *Skepticism* has become an ingrained disposition or even a virtue. If no one can be trusted, the

> One of the real problems in corporate America today is that the corporation has become a machine. People go to work and they sit in cubicles, and they have no sense of meaning.
>
> *Merrill Oster,*
> *business journalist*

intelligent response to a person who claims to know the truth is to question assumptions and challenge assertions.

A few years ago I (Bill) traveled to Poland to speak at a youth conference. One evening the students presented a program for outsiders. After a beautiful pantomime presenting Jesus' death, resurrection, and offer of salvation, two students told their personal faith stories and asked if anyone wanted to follow Jesus. A woman blurted out in Polish, "This is just priest talk." It wasn't a compliment. This woman dismissed the Christian message because she didn't trust priests. Sadly, her abrupt dismissal of truth is not uncommon.

Perhaps the most insidious effect of postmodernism is the *despair* and *cynicism* it leaves in its wake. The "been there, done that" attitude has left a vacuum of purposelessness—manifested by the increasingly common brush-off term *whatever*. Left with nothing outside of one's self to define meaning, the postmodern mind finds no compelling idea to live for. Internally defined purpose has no power. When we are off-mission, our lives fall apart.

The Upside of Postmodernism

Those of us who are concerned about the eternal destiny of our work colleagues can be encouraged that not all the news is bad. Consider these positives:

- Overconfidence in human reason is being corrected. Postmodernists agree with Christians that science, technology, and politics cannot solve humankind's most basic problems.
- Spirituality is increasingly acceptable and welcome. Skepticism toward the supernatural is waning. Surveys show that most Americans claim to be more open to spiritual things than at almost any other time in history. However, most of them are looking for spiritual truth outside of Christianity.
- The importance of relationships is being rediscovered. Postmodernists agree with the Bible that people are more than biological machines and that community and connection with others is vitally important. This emphasis on relationships was accelerated by the tragedy of September 11, 2001, on United States soil.

THE OPPORTUNITY

Although many Christians are nervous about the impact of post-modernism, we can be sure that God is not distressed. A postmodern culture provides a huge opportunity for us to retell a key part of our story that had been lost in the age of modernism. Although people may believe that religion is a myth, they are starving for meaning and for something that brings order and purpose to their lives. They have found themselves with no treatment for the guilt they experience and no antidote for the lack of satisfaction.

A decreasing number of people are willing these days to go to an evangelistic crusade, but most will respond to a relationship. People want to know a person, not a message. God's main method of evangelism has always been personal. According to George Barna, half of adults are annoyed when a *stranger* tries to share his or her faith with them, but this same group is not annoyed when close friends, loving neighbors, or trusted associates have a spiritual conversation with them.[9] People don't necessarily want to hear you preach a sermon or have you hand them a gospel tract, but they do want to see and hear about what God is doing in their friend's life.

When our message of what Jesus can do for a person is limited to the afterlife, we not only miss a major part of the gospel message, but we also lose our audience. People are concerned about the quality of their lives. They want a God who's good for today, not just in the hereafter — a God who can handle their needs, dreams, hurts, disappointments, and failures right now.

If your God isn't interested in the details and dilemmas of everyday life, then you've got a hard sell. Happily, this isn't the case. We have a God who approaches us with a "what's in it for you" attitude. He never says to us, "Ask not what your God can do for you; ask what you can do for your God." This is what he declares, as recorded by the apostle John:

> This is how God showed his love among us: He sent his one and only Son into the world that we might live through him. This is love: not that we loved God, but that he loved us and sent his Son as an atoning sacrifice for our sins.
>
> 1 John 4:9 – 10

During the 1960s and 1970s the church hemorrhaged young people. In the 1980s these rebels began to return in equal numbers. But by the 1990s, church had been tried and found wanting. The church, it appeared, was promising more than it delivered. It was long on taking and short on giving what people wanted—relationships, purpose, and wisdom to handle life.

If we give people the impression that all we care about is what they can do for the church, we will very likely lose our audience. And rightly so, for God's request to serve him is always based on what he has already done for us, not on what we can do for him. We make a mistake when we forget that non-Christians have no hope of any other attitude except self-centeredness before they know the life-changing power of Jesus.

God does care about these things. He cares about more, to be sure, but don't miss the fact that *what people want, Jesus has to offer*—not to meet their basest greed but their most basic longings. Are people hungry? Absolutely! Can we feed them? Yes, if we're willing to discover what they really want, and then *show* them— not just tell them—how Jesus can meet these needs—and all the needs of our lives.

THE BOTTOM LINE										

As Christians, we have what people want. And we need to learn how to communicate in ways they can understand.

EARNING THE RIGHT
TO BE HEARD

In his parable of the sower (Matthew 13), Jesus does not paint a pretty picture of the human heart. Hard-packed soil, weeds, and rocks all thwart the seed of the word of God from penetrating and bearing the intended fruit. Just as every farmer must overcome obstacles to produce a crop, men and women who want to see eternal life spring up in the lives of their coworkers face a human heart full of emotional, intellectual, and volitional barriers that must be faced before the seed of faith can take root and grow into eternal life.

Our words alone, no matter how wise or eloquent, cannot overcome these obstacles. God's method of preparing human hearts for his message usually involves personal contacts with people of faith who display the character of Jesus in their day-to-day lives. Exposure to a person of godly character can soften the soil of the heart and create a desire to hear what we have to say.

IT BEGINS WITH THE HEART

Jane was a new customer who was switching the maintenance of her company's security service to Bob's company. As Bob interviewed Jane about her needs, she mentioned that she had been offended by the owner and employees of her former service. Surprised by Jane's display of emotion, Bob asked, "What did the owner do?"

Jane paused and then confided, almost in a whisper, "He asked me, in front of his staff and another customer, if I was a Christian. I was mortified."

Bob, a follower of Jesus, active in a local church, sensed that he needed to be very careful. "Wow," he commented, "was that a surprise?"

"Surprise!" she exclaimed. "How dare he ask such a private question in a public setting. I knew right then and there I didn't want to use that business anymore!"

Bob sensed a quiet voice inside, prompting him to explore this display of emotion. "I sense that spirituality or religion is of concern to you."

Jane looked at him suspiciously and answered in a hostile tone, "No! I never want to see another religious business owner again after the way I was treated."

Bob continued his questioning. "Was it just his comment that was offensive to you?"

"Heavens, no!" she blurted out. "They had this art with Bible verses all over the walls and they played taped organ music—but worst of all, they were rude every time I came in." She took a deep breath. "You won't believe what he did the *last* time I was in. He asked me if I knew where I would spend eternity if I were to die that night. I tell you, that really scared me. I mean, it would scare anyone. Then he tried to talk to me about Jesus—right in front of other people. That scared me even more. I'll never do business with a religious business owner again."

It doesn't matter how knowledgeable you are in the things of God, how skilled you are at persuasion, how adept at apologetics you are, or how convincingly you craft your arguments. The pathway to becoming a person of spiritual influence always begins with address-

> I felt called in my work to be a light. So someone said, why don't we just do an acrostic around *light* for our statement of purpose?
>
> **L** Lead by example
> **I** Invest in others, in employees
> **G** Give freely
> **H** Honor God
> **T** Treat all business contacts with respect
>
> I feel compelled to be the light. Light doesn't speak, it simply shines. I want to be someone who influences people in the business world by my character. And my character needs to be lined up with Jesus Christ.
>
> *Anne Beiler, food service*

ing the issues of the heart. You can't hope to influence non-Christians if an emotional barrier has hardened the soil of their hearts.

SOIL ANALYSIS

Almost every pre-Christian has emotional barriers—issues that harden the heart, keep spiritual truth at arm's length, and sometimes lead to the pursuit of counterfeit forms of spirituality. A person with emotional barriers won't be open to or able to hear what you say, much less to respond to your overtures.

We define *emotional barriers* as "negative sentiments—denial, indifference, mistrust, antagonism, and fear—toward Christianity (or Christians) that a person has come to accept as true." They are usually based on negative experiences with Christians or religious groups. These sentiments are not unique, of course, to the United States. A citizen of another country recently told me (Bill) that 70 percent of the people in his country thought that going to church would increase their stress and anxiety (based on a poll of the citizens).

There are a number of circumstances that can cause emotional barriers. Exposure to narrow-minded or judgmental religious groups or people can breed contempt. Invitations to repent and pleas to "turn or burn" not only fall on deaf ears when the call is not experienced in a context of love and compassion, but they create emotional barriers of anger, bitterness, and indifference toward Christianity. By not being sensitive and loving when dispensing the truth, well-meaning Christians who believe they should aggressively present the gospel to strangers have "damaged fruit," often without realizing it.

Television evangelists who lack integrity and strong moral character have spawned mistrust in a highly visible way. But celebrity preachers certainly have no corner on emotional damage. In those instances where a community's spiritual leaders (as well as high-profile laypersons) violate trust or fall into public sin, much damage can be done to the cause of the gospel because of the fiduciary responsibility that comes with the position. James warns of the strict judgment that comes on those in positions of high influence: "Not many of you should presume to be teachers, my brothers, because you know that we who teach will be judged more strictly" (James 3:1).

Hypocrisy may well be the trait in Christians that has turned hearts away from Jesus more quickly than just about anything else. Hypocritical parents, relatives, neighbors, teachers, spiritual leaders, coworkers, and bosses do incalculable damage to the cause of the gospel. Here's a case in point. Jim grew up in the slums of a major city. He attended church for the first time when a bus picked up gang members to take them to a youth service. Jim was attracted to the people at church and went regularly. He was looking for answers to life's problems that neither his parents nor friends could give him. It wasn't long before two deacons got into an ugly public dispute that split the church. Because of the rancorous behavior of these men, Jim walked away, convinced that the love he had experienced was fake. He didn't set foot in a church again for three decades.

Many people are indifferent toward Christianity because they've been bored by what they saw and experienced at church. By age eight Susan had concluded that the church she attended with her parents didn't have anything she needed. When old enough to make her own decision, she opted not to go to church—for thirty-five years. Like Susan, millions of men and women who attended church as children have now concluded that Christianity isn't relevant. Oh, maybe church was nice, but who needs one more *nice* thing to do?

SOIL TREATMENT

Will rational arguments pacify negative emotions? Will preaching or biblical exposition reduce anger or bitterness? Will persuasion penetrate a hard heart? Perhaps, but not as often as you may wish. However, a nonmanipulative relationship with *you*—where a non-Christian respects you and experiences love and acceptance—can plow through even the hardest soil. The groundwork for this day-to-day ministry in the workplace always starts with the condition of *our* own hearts—not the hearts of our coworkers.

This stage in the evangelism process is the cultivation phase. The specific focus here is the *heart*, not the head. The goal of the cultivation phase is to earn a person's trust. If a person does not trust us, he or she will never trust what we say about Jesus. This trust—in both cases—is built on several things, including our professional competence, our godly character, and our personal compassion. It is *not* built on communication skills or evangelistic techniques. As this trust develops, our colleagues and friends will want to know more about what makes us different, and eventually they will want to know more about the God we serve.

> Our own deep personal faith is the first priority. God makes this promise: "Draw near to me, and I will draw near to you." So I try to draw near so that God will shine through me. I pray about it a lot, and I do every bit I can to live it so that people can see a living witness.
>
> *Norm Miller,*
> *automotive supply*

Sadly, trust has become a rare commodity in the workplace. Less than half of the workers surveyed a decade ago trusted top management, and only one-third thought their employers treated them with dignity and respect.[1] With the recent deluge of corporate scandals, trust has diminished even more.

Trust is not self-generating in non-Christians—or in anyone, for that matter. It's a response to our character and action. It must be earned. In the next section we'll consider the five traits we must exhibit and act on if we expect people to trust us and allow us to influence them.

FIVE ESSENTIALS FOR SPIRITUAL INFLUENCE IN THE WORKPLACE

Influence is the power or capacity to produce a desired result, to impact, or to cause some change to take place. Rather than focusing on laws, influence focuses on hearts. Although laws and influence both involve power, the power of influence is not imposed but granted willingly. Influence, as a result, changes people from within. It sways their thoughts, their perceptions, and their values—changing the soil of their hearts from the inside out. As a result, influence also has the power to change behavior.

Where does this kind of power come from? We may be tempted to assume that the influence is in our position. Yes, some careers today (professional sports and medicine, for example) provide more opportunities for influence than, say, plumbing. But there is more to being influential than having an MD behind your name. A plumber can be more influential than a doctor when the following five essentials come together:

1. SPIRITUAL INFLUENCE REQUIRES COMPETENCE

People are often surprised at this proposition, which we emphasize at our conferences: The *foundational* requirement for spiritual influence is competence—the pursuit of excellence in one's daily work. By excellence and competence we don't mean to imply that you have to be better than everyone else. It does mean, however, that you are serious about doing good work—about doing your best.

> If we are out there being spiritual and then doing a very poor job at what we do, it negates the spiritual truth we are trying to disseminate.
>
> *Larry Collett,*
> *information technology*

What does the Bible say? We've already noted the command in Colossians 3:23 to work "with all your heart." Ecclesiastes 9:10 says, "Whatever your hand finds to do, do it with all your might." Proverbs 22:29 states, "Do you see a man skilled in his work? He will serve before kings; he will not serve before obscure men." When it comes to doing good work, Vince Lombardi and the Bible concur. The Hall of Fame professional football coach once said, "The quality of a person's life is in direct proportion to their commitment to excellence, regardless of their chosen field of endeavor."

Consider the impact the Old Testament character Daniel had on the kings he served. Had Daniel performed in a mediocre manner in his job, it's doubtful we would know of him today, no matter how godly he might have been. Look at what Nebuchadnezzar noted when he interviewed Daniel and his friends at the end of their education: "In every matter of wisdom and understanding about which the king questioned them, he found them ten times better than all the magicians and enchanters in his whole kingdom" (Daniel 1:20).

Seventy years later, King Darius discovered the same extraordinary competence: "Now Daniel so distinguished himself among the administrators and the satraps by his exceptional qualities that the king planned to set him over the whole kingdom" (Daniel 6:3).

Consider Jesus himself. Can you imagine him using substandard materials, doing shoddy carpentry work, or overcharging his customers? Picture a former customer sitting in the audience after Jesus began his ministry. If he had done poor work, can't you imagine someone turning a deaf ear and muttering, "I'm not listening to this guy anymore. I can't trust him. The table he built for me fell apart after only one year"? An intelligent person might conclude that Jesus' theology was only as reliable as his tables. I can imagine that the tables and benches

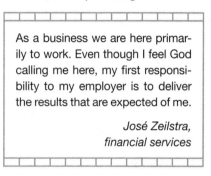

As a business we are here primarily to work. Even though I feel God calling me here, my first responsibility to my employer is to deliver the results that are expected of me.

José Zeilstra,
financial services

Jesus made were collectors' items for generations—not only because of who he was but also because of the quality of his craftsmanship.

Again, we're not saying that we have to be star players. We don't have to be *the* best, but we do have to give *our* best. Here is the fundamental principle: If we want people to pay attention to our faith, we must first pay attention to our work. Before we introduce coworkers to God, we must introduce God into our work.

Competence Requires Natural Ability

What each person needs to ask is not "What do I want to do, and what do I have to do to get there?" but "Who am I? Who has God designed me to be, and how do I develop what God has already put in me?" Competence isn't only the result of diligence, effort, or hard work. It demands *natural ability*. As God created each of us with a unique inventory of abilities, he had our function—our unique calling—in mind. By discovering our design, we uncover the mystery of our calling. God's will—the place of my greatest fulfillment and joy, greatest competence, and greatest influence—is essentially being what he made me to be.

It's our job, then, to discover, submit to, and develop these gifts. Only then will we develop the competence to be the influence God created us to be—no matter what level of influence he has in mind for us. When we have this influence, the effects are dramatic.

Competence Requires Discipline

God may give the gifts, but we must still choose to discover, develop, and employ these gifts. Culture may provide us the opportunity to touch vast numbers of people, but we must still choose to endure the discipline of craftsmanship to seize the opportunity. This is not news to anyone who's endured a tough career-training program.

> To be excellent and work hard and be diligent because that is what you are getting paid to do is a language the world understands. I was disappointed, being a CEO of a company for so many years, that oftentimes non-Christians would take their work more seriously and outwork Christians.
>
> *Jack Alexander, travel and hospitality industry*

Daniel and his friends were gifted intellectually, and they possessed great ability in administrating, serving, and organizing. But all this was not enough. To hone their skills, they humbly endured three grueling years of disciplined study. Daniel was faithful to develop what God had given him, and in the ancient Near East he became perhaps the most enduring political influence of his generation.

2. SPIRITUAL INFLUENCE REQUIRES CHARACTER

But competence is only part of the influence equation. It's not enough to be good at what you do. *Great character* must govern great giftedness if we want to maintain any influence gained by our competent work. Lack of integrity and character has aborted the influence of many a leader. Richard Nixon and Bill Clinton are two who come to mind—brilliant, competent men with flaws that diminished their influence.

On the other side are figures like Billy Graham and C. Everett Koop, whose integrity has compelled even their toughest ideological critics to respect and admire them. Authentic character—Christlike character—consistently impresses people. It engages attention and influences people because God designed men and women to admire the virtue and character traits God possesses. Unbelieving men and women who were repulsed by the religious people of the first century were attracted to Jesus. Why? Because whenever they observed him, they saw the traits described in Galatians 5:22—love, joy, peace, patience, kindness, goodness, faithfulness, gentleness, and self-control.

God's call to each of us also includes a transformation in which we are conformed into the image of Jesus—a destination we move toward in a number of ways, the most important of which is through intimacy with Jesus himself. Simply put, the more time I spend in intimate communication with Jesus, the more he influences me—the more his character rubs off on me. My old life is being exchanged for his new life. The more this balance shifts—my old life for his new life—the more like Jesus I become.

When we exhibit peace, love, and joy, we are magnetic. Patience, kindness, goodness, faithfulness, gentleness, and self-control speak loudly that we are people who can be trusted. Even if people hate what we believe, over time they will be attracted by Jesus' character reflected in us.

Repeatedly throughout the day you can ask, "What would Jesus do if he were in my workplace? How would he respond to this situation?" When competence and character—character like that of Jesus—link up in us, they produce a palpable authority, impact, and influence.

3. SPIRITUAL INFLUENCE REQUIRES CONSIDERATION

Nothing reveals more about your character than how you treat people. It may be a cliché, but it is one packed with truth: People don't care how much we know until they know how much we care. Character is not just something we are internally; it expresses itself outwardly in the thoughtfulness we display to others—our tenderness and compassion, our mercy and kindness, our attentiveness and gentleness.

Consideration is the logical result of receiving grace. If we ever find ourselves being harsh with someone, it's because we've lost the sense of God's graciousness to us. Paul reminds us of this in his letter to the Philippian believers:

> If you have any encouragement from being united with Christ, if any comfort from his love, if any fellowship with the Spirit, if any tenderness and compassion, then make my joy complete by being like-minded, having the same love, being one in spirit and purpose. Do nothing out of selfish ambition or vain conceit, but in humility consider others better than yourselves. Each of you should look not only to your own interests, but also to the interests of others.
>
> Philippians 2:1–4

Consideration Involves Our Communication

One of the most accurate measures of consideration can be taken by watching people talk about other people in the break room or at lunch. What do they say? How do they say it?

Now turn the mirror on yourself. What do you say about others when they are not in your presence? Do you gossip? Do you denigrate, deprecate, disparage, ridicule, or belittle? The apostle Paul gives us little wiggle room: "Do not let any unwholesome talk come out of your mouths, but only what is helpful for building others up according to their needs, that it may benefit those who listen" (Ephesians 4:29). Is this your standard of speech?

If you are a leader, communication that engenders trust involves a lot more than avoiding cutting remarks, abusive tongue-lashings, or other fear-based tactics of management. It involves creating an atmosphere that fosters the free and

> God asks us to do things in a kingdom way that's often quite different from the way things are done here on earth. We have to recognize the tension between well-rounded lives and quarterly earnings. Our focus is going to have to be on the hearts and the well-being of people. That is going to put us in conflict with some business goals and objectives at times.
>
> *Larry Collett,*
> *information technology*

open exchange of information and keeps people up-to-date on key issues that affect their work. In his chapter titled "Rebuilding Trust in the Fractured Workplace," dispute-resolution attorney Carlton Snow makes this observation:

> The greater the amount of authentic communication, the higher the likelihood that an atmosphere of trust will develop. The ease of communication at work is as important as the amount of communication. In most American workplaces, for example, information is shared on a need-to-know basis, but a more open pattern of sharing information will engender greater trust.[2]

Keeping people who work for you "in the know" shows personal respect and trust, reduces suspicion, and invites trust. If someone doesn't trust you as his or her boss, that person will not trust you in spiritual matters either.

The same principle holds true if you are the one reporting to a boss or supervisor. Trust is a two-way street. Never think you cannot have influence, including spiritual influence, on those who are higher than you on the corporate ladder. And never underestimate the value to a supervisor of overseeing employees he or she can trust.

> I feel responsible to be a spiritual influence in my workplace in many ways. One of them is by being good to the employees and exceeding their expectations. If your light is going to shine, your actions should confirm what you say. If your actions don't confirm what you say, then you confuse those around you.
>
> *Anne Beiler, food service*

Consideration Involves Our Listening

Carlton Snow pinpoints a key issue for those of us who want to express great character in our outward actions: "If communication is at the heart of building trust, listening is its lifeblood."[3] Failure to listen ultimately indicates a lack of respect—whether you are discussing a knotty business problem or talking about a spiritual principle. Those who listen while also exhibiting a humble spirit

and deep commitment to fellow employees invite trust and cooperation in business and in personal relationships. Those who go out
of their way to listen to and get input from others send a powerful
message to coworkers: "I trust you. I care what you think. You have
something valuable to contribute to me. I'm depending on you. You
are invaluable."

Good listeners don't just hear the words; they also seek to understand the speaker. They clarify and reflect back what they hear to
be sure they've heard accurately. They aim not to become defensive
if comments or feedback hit too close to home. While listening they
aren't busy formulating what to say in return. They will look into
the eyes—and the souls—of the person who is speaking to them.

Consideration Involves Our Actions

Communication and conduct—these two relational components
must go together. Jointly they send a powerful message to the people
with whom we work. The
way in which we respond to
circumstances—the way we
live—tells people we either
care more about ourselves
and our own selfish agendas
or we care more about others and can be trusted. Being
trustworthy opens the door
for our messages to be heard
and heeded, whether they are
business- or faith-related.

> Part of our outward call is legiti-
> mately loving people and meet-
> ing the needs of people where
> they are. I am very cautious when
> I think about evangelism in the
> workplace, because I always ask
> myself if I have earned the right
> with this person. Have I demon-
> strated Christian love in this re-
> lationship and have I earned the
> right to share Christ with them?
>
> *Jack Alexander, travel and
> hospitality industry*

The experience of a phy-
sician friend illustrates this
point. John is an excellent
internist whose character
was put on public display as he established his practice. While dealing with the normal professional stresses on a young doctor, John
and his wife had their first child, a son born with spina bifida. John's
colleagues were well aware of the strain on him as he managed his
workload while making frequent trips to Texas Children's Hospital.

John may have had reason to be irritable, but he rarely was. One day during rounds, he discovered that a nurse had made a serious mistake that endangered a patient's life. John reprimanded the nurse firmly but respectfully. She walked away with her self-respect intact—an unusual result when compared with similar encounters with unhappy doctors. John was unaware that a colleague had overheard his reprimand. Leaving the nursing station, John felt a hand on his shoulder. "John," his colleague said, "I overheard how you handled that situation. If you were a preacher, I'd go to your church."

The fact is, John is a preacher. You are, too, and so are we. When people see our competence, character, and consideration, the things we say have a power equal to or greater than any sermon preached from a pulpit. There is a distance between pulpit and pew that does not exist in the workplace.

4. SPIRITUAL INFLUENCE REQUIRES WISE COMMUNICATION

We often meet people who tell us they're uncomfortable talking about their faith in the workplace. Some feel guilty about it. Others have decided they can witness without ever saying a word. We believe, however, that deeds without words are usually just as ineffective as words without deeds.

Theologian Elton Trublood concluded that people who declare they can witness to their faith purely by their deeds are insufferably self-righteous—no one is *that* good. The apostle Peter reminds us that we need to be ready to speak: "But in your hearts set apart Christ as Lord. Always be prepared to give an answer to everyone who asks you to give the reason for the hope that you have. But do this with gentleness and respect" (1 Peter 3:15).

Peter's words also give us a clue that there may be times to keep our mouths shut. Aggressive evangelists zero in on the word "always" while sometimes overlooking the fact that there is a condition given here. We are to be ready to give an answer to "everyone who asks." Ambushing an uninterested person with the gospel may give some Christians a rush, but it's not productive, nor is it biblical in our estimation. There are times when it's appropriate and times when it's inappropriate to talk about our faith. Obviously, it takes wisdom to know the difference.

A few years ago I (Bill) was talking with a professor at a major university. This committed Christian had carved out an important place of leadership. Because this university had a reputation for cultivating a "politically correct" environment and was less than warm toward evangelical theology, I was curious to know how he negotiated the conflict between his faith and the pressures of academia. I said to him, "I guess you have to be careful about sharing your faith here."

He looked at me with a puzzled expression. "No," he said, "I don't have to be careful." He paused. "But I do have to be wise."

I got the point. When Jesus sent his disciples out to preach the gospel, he said, "I am sending you out like sheep among wolves. Therefore be as shrewd as snakes and as innocent as doves" (Matthew 10:16). The Greek word translated "shrewd" means "thoughtful" or "discreet." Jesus uses this word's positive side to remind us to think before we speak. Our motives must be pure and our methods wise and appropriate. When is it appropriate? Here is what we suggest:

1. It's fitting to talk about your faith *when it arises out of relationships naturally built around your work with another person.* As you discuss work and life with your coworkers, informal mention of spiritual truth will happen naturally, just as other topics of personal importance pop into your conversation. In chapter 6 we'll illustrate this principle and explain how to use faith flags and faith stories in conversations at work.

2. It's appropriate to talk about your faith *when it naturally fits into the topic of conversation.* That is to say, your conversation should be organic, not mechanical—not contrived, not crafted or calculated to divert discussion into another totally unrelated area. You may have observed people who drop the evangelistic "diagnostic question" out of the blue after a lunch with a colleague: "If you died tonight and stood before the gates of heaven, and God asked you why he should let you in, what would you say?" This can have a chilling effect on a conversation—as well as on a budding relationship.

3. It's always appropriate to talk about your faith *when you are asked.* A question is an open door to address a person's spiritual concern. It is not, however, an invitation to dump all

of your spiritual knowledge on someone in one sitting. Give enough information to answer a person's question, but also be sure to look for ways to create more curiosity and questions that can be addressed as time goes on.

5. Spiritual Influence Requires Courage

Centuries ago, the philosopher Tacitus noted, "The desire for safety stands against every great and noble endeavor." If living a quiet life of personal peace and prosperity is more compelling to us than following Jesus, we will be unwilling to put our lives on the line.

Whether it's taking a step toward having more public influence or mustering the courage to answer a coworker's spiritual question, following Jesus is anything but a safe venture. You will meet opportunities and face obstacles that will challenge you to the edge of your faith. Remember that true safety is in *following Jesus* wherever he leads. But playing it safe is the most dangerous thing you can do if Jesus is leading you out of your comfort zone.

Courage Comes from a Close Walk with God

A close walk with God is the only antidote to fear. The Lord commanded Joshua, "Be strong and courageous. Do not be terrified; do not be discouraged, for the LORD your God will be with you wherever you go" (Joshua 1:9). When the heart is gripped by fear, the soul is frozen by inertia. When God grips the heart, the soul is free to risk great things for his kingdom.

Courage Comes from Absorbing the Truth of God's Word

As Joshua prepared to lead Israel into Canaan, God said, "Do not let this Book of the Law depart from your mouth; meditate on it day and night" (Joshua 1:8). Jesus said to his followers, "If you hold to my teaching, you are really my disciples. Then you will know the truth, and the truth will set you free" (John 8:31–32).

There is a direct relationship between courage and the Scriptures. God's Word fortifies us with the truth. It gives us the mental ammunition to do battle with the lies of Satan that threaten to make us fall back in fear. Knowing that God is with us wherever we go gives us the courage to resist the fear and discouragement that Satan will undoubtedly throw in our path as we pursue God's will and walk the path of competence, character, compassion, and courage. Ultimately these steps of courage, when rooted in an abiding knowledge of the Word of God, result in true, satisfying, and abundant freedom to become all that God made us to be.

Courage Comes from Others

God is the One who gives his people courage to travel toward their destiny. But he has also designed us to benefit from hearing a good, affirming, and encouraging word from fellow believers.

That's what *encouragement* is all about: putting courage into someone else's heart. Again and again in small groups I've heard someone speak just the right word or Scripture that inspired courage, conviction, or conduct in another person's battle. One person can make a difference, but we are not designed to operate alone. More times than not, the one who has the courage to stand and change history has one or more advocates, defenders, or prayer partners who bring encouragement when fear creeps in to steal all sense of God's presence.

THE CHALLENGE

We don't know exactly how God has designed you or what your destiny in his plan may be. We don't know what God has put on and in your heart, but we challenge you to reach for it. No matter how improbable or impossible it appears, if it is noble, right, pure, and in line with God's kingdom, you must stretch yourself to reach it. To do less would be tragic for you, your customers, clients, and coworkers, for your profession, and for our generation—but most of all for the kingdom.

THE BOTTOM LINE											

If we want people to pay attention to our faith, we must pay attention to the kind of people we are.

5

KEEP IT SIMPLE

In his book *The Circle of Innovation*, business guru Tom Peters describes a trip he took:

> My first stop was the Ritz Carlton at Peachtree Center in Atlanta. In the course of my stay, I encountered 25 to 30 hotel employees. Some were housekeepers … some were waiters … some were maintenance people … some were accountants on their way to meetings with sheaves of paper under their arms.
>
> Every one of them (including the accountants!) performed what I call The Ritz Pause. That is, they took a couple of seconds, stopped, looked me in the eye, and asked, "How's everything going? Is there anything I can do for you?"[1]

When it comes to gaining and retaining customers, don't count on glitzy lobbies and brass doodads. According to Peters, "Little things = strategic advantage." It's the small *common courtesies* that keep people coming back for more. Actions that take only a few seconds make a huge difference. Peters believes it is superior customer service with a "slavish devotion" to detail that makes a company truly exceptional. Pretty simple when you come right down to it.

Yet many companies continue to concentrate on the "big things" without realizing that it's the simple things that keep customers coming back. I (Bill) have had the privilege of visiting the corporate headquarters of Southwest Airlines, which has a reputation for quality customer care. Colleen Barrett, Southwest Airlines president and chief operating officer, knows how to find the right people. She outlines their employment criteria: "listening, caring, smiling, saying 'thank you,' and being warm." No wonder Southwest is almost always at or near the top of the Department of Transportation's list for fewest customer complaints.[2]

There are Christians, too, who think that the big things matter most when it comes to spiritual influence. Rather than focusing on simple common courtesies, they believe one needs bold actions, overt spiritual conversations, and highly persuasive arguments or witnessing techniques to influence people spiritually. We disagree. We've seen that this emphasis on big things can keep Christians on the sidelines. According to George Barna's research, only about 12 percent of Christians consider themselves specially gifted for outreach.[3] Most of us aren't wired to be a Billy Graham or Bill Bright, yet we feel some pressure to be "great evangelists." Deluded into thinking we're second-class Christians if we don't emulate the techniques of the great evangelists, we're tempted to park our faith outside the workplace where it's safe, which means it will be of little benefit to anyone, including us.

As a senior in college, Jim received an offer from a national accounting firm. He had done well in school and had been a leader with a college ministry that trained him in the techniques of cold-contact evangelism. He had become pretty comfortable knocking on the dorm doors of strangers to discuss their spiritual condition.

Jim believed that God gave him the accounting job to use as a witnessing platform to bring people into God's kingdom. He said, "I was so excited to be placed in a building with several hundred non-Christians. Many missionaries in foreign countries weren't in as wonderful a situation as I was. So I witnessed from the first day of my job—during staff training and at lunch. I'd even spend my break time going from cubicle to cubicle. I literally had mapped out the whole firm, just as I had mapped out dorms in college. I set a goal of witnessing to every employee during that first year. There were nearly a thousand employees in the firm, which meant I needed to share my faith only four times a day. And, given my experience in college, I fully expected a quarter of them to pray with me to receive Christ."

Imagine Jim's surprise when, after only a month of employment, his supervisor told him that his position was being terminated. His job performance was superior, but there were just too many complaints about the foisting of his beliefs on others who ended up being offended.

As Jim told his story, he lowered his head. "I was shocked. I was angry at the company for firing me. I was angry at my colleagues for not letting me know how they felt but instead gossiping and complaining behind my back. I was angry at God for allowing it to happen."

Now, years later, no one in his workplace knows that he is a Christian and an active church member. He learned his lesson the hard way, and he now believes that "the workplace is no place for evangelism."

Jim's problem was that he failed to recognize that the practice of evangelism must fit the environment. Generally speaking, what you can get away with on the college campus is quite different from "real life." When it comes to the workplace, we are not called to bring people to Jesus but rather to bring Jesus to people. And given the cultural and legal realities of the business world, Christians today must bring Jesus to people in ways that are appropriate and relevant, both to the office environment and to individual employees.

BEING A WITNESS VERSUS WITNESSING

Besides the fact that one is a noun and the other a verb, there is a world of difference between *witnessing* and being a *witness*. John Fischer writes in *Fearless Faith*: "It would save a lot of time and embarrassment if we could learn one thing about witnessing and evangelism: Salvation is God's thing and is out of our control. Saving people is God's part, ours is being a witness."[4]

Witnessing (the verb) is mechanical. Do this, say that—and if you do it right, the person prays the prayer. Success or failure rests pretty much on me. But being a witness (the noun) is organic. We cultivate, plant, and water, but we are as dependent on God for the harvest as any farmer.

People are often surprised to learn that the term *witnessing* is not in the Bible, yet the word *witness* permeates the New Testament. Nowhere are we told to *go witnessing*.

Virtually every deviation of modern evangelistic theory from the biblical process of evangelism involves changing the noun *witness* to the verb *witnessing*, separating who we are from what we say and do. Someone may ask us, "Did you witness at work today?" (or the variant, "Did you share your faith this week?"). John Fischer makes this observation:

When witnessing is a verb, it becomes something we do or don't do. We turn it on or we turn it off. It becomes a segment of the spiritual compartment of our lives, as in prayer, Bible study, going to church, and witnessing—a very small segment. It's something we are supposed to go out and do, and poor, unsuspecting non-Christians often have to bear the brunt of our spiritual obligation.[5]

If it is valid (and we believe it is) to say we've tended to over-emphasize witnessing as something we do, the relevant question should be, "Are you a witness?" Whether we like it or not, the answer is yes. The reality all too often, though, is that our witness (our life) says one thing while our witnessing (our words) says another. Many non-Christians with whom we interact share a common emotional obstacle to Christianity: They have been turned off by well-meaning Christians who have witnessed to them. These Christians weren't nearly as interested in discovering what God was doing in a person's life as they were in what *they* were supposed to do to fulfill their obligation. They had made the non-Christian a project, not a friend. And in the process, obstacles went up and trust went down. When we concentrate on witnessing rather than on being a witness, we're asking a person to take an impossibly big leap rather than small incremental steps toward Jesus. If we forget the little things, it becomes all about us—not about God and what he wants. It's about our success, not a person's spiritual welfare.

John Fischer again helps us see what can happen when we focus on witnessing as something we do:

> Witnessing ... tends to make us goal-oriented, opening the door to results, expectations, and, ultimately, the numbers game. With witnessing there are corners of cards to tear off, hands to raise, numbers to tally, reports to make. Witnessing is all one-way. *We* witness. *We* talk. *We* say what we came to say and try to make people listen to us. Such witnessing can have only two results: You either "pray the prayer" or you don't. And in the end, our witnessing can be judged as a success or a failure based on one response at one point in time.[6]

These attempts to witness expose a basic misunderstanding of biblical evangelism, namely, that we are the responsible agents of salvation to our friends who don't know God. Jesus dispelled this myth when he taught, "No one can come to me unless the Father who sent me draws him" (John 6:44). We are not God's recruiters or headhunters. It's not our job to "close the sale" or "get them to sign on the dotted line."

EXPERT OR MATERIAL WITNESS?

We are called to *be* witnesses—to show and tell what we have seen and what we know. We are to be witnesses of the way that God, through faith, prayer, and the Bible, has transformed our lives. This is what we're to pass on to others through simple, daily interaction: how God has given us hope and joy, meaning and significance, and how biblical principles help us solve or cope with day-to-day problems and troubles.

A close friend of ours (both authors), Bob Snyder, MD, founder of International Health Services, wrote about this concept in an email devotional.[7] He explained that as an emergency physician, he sometimes went to court in one of two capacities—either as a material witness or as an expert witness:

> As a material witness, I was asked to give an account of what had happened to me, what I had seen and heard. When I was a material witness, there was never anyone testifying against me. My credentials as a physician were not an issue; only the truthful expression of what I observed was necessary.
>
> Serving as an expert witness was an entirely different matter. Both the prosecution and defense examined my credentials and had to agree that I was an "expert." Then I gave an opinion about the events of a case in which I was never involved. As soon as I finished my testimony, another physician was often called who frequently gave contradictory testimony. Truth, at times, did not seem to be the issue, but rather who could be the most convincing.

Thinking of these distinctions in terms of his faith, Bob eventually realized that God certainly wants some of us to give expert witness concerning him. The evidence for the claims of Jesus, he noted, is overwhelming. But for most of us, said Bob, our primary responsibility is as a material witness. Consider the story of the man who had been blind since birth. After his healing by Jesus, he was a *material witness* to the Pharisees when he said, "I was blind but now I see!" (John 9:25). The Pharisees tried to get him to be an *expert witness*, but he refused. He testified about who had healed him and about the fact that he had been healed. He simply told his story and left the results up to God.

Witnessing assumes that the results are up to us; *being a witness* assumes that the results are up to God. Note what Jesus said to his disciples: "On account of me you will stand before governors and kings as witnesses to them.... Do not worry beforehand about what to say. Just say whatever is given you at the time, for it is not you speaking, but the Holy Spirit" (Mark 13:9, 11). What an amazing promise! In biblical evangelism, there's nothing you have to memorize, no techniques or sales pitches to practice, no complicated philosophical arguments to comprehend and communicate. It's just telling your story naturally, in the midst of the many divine appointments the Lord gives you each day. In the biblical sense, a witness does not always witness, but a witness *is* always a witness who shows others what Jesus has done and is doing in his or her life.

We suspect that this failure to understand the difference between being an expert witness and being a material witness, or the difference between witnessing and being a witness, is one of the reasons most Christians think they can't be a person of spiritual influence anywhere, much less in their workplace. In fact, being an effective witness is as easy as inviting a coworker to have a cup of coffee.

COMMON COURTESIES

We've co-opted Tom Peters's customer-service term *common courtesies* to describe the small acts of kindness that can build up over time to create spiritual capital in a relationship. These acts can pave the way for more in-depth spiritual conversation later — with you or with the next "witness" God plans to use in this person's spiritual journey. As you read these next paragraphs, we hope you'll marvel at just how easy it is to perform acts of common courtesy and go on to say with us, "I can do that!"

COMMON COURTESIES ARE ORDINARY

Common courtesies are everyday acts of kindness. They are a "cup of cold water" (Matthew 10:42) given in Jesus' name. In a day when basic civility is often lacking, common courtesies speak volumes, and the fact that acts of kindness are unexpected gives them power. Common courtesies include actions such as:

- remembering an employee's, customer's, or client's name — and their spouse's name, too
- remembering an employee's, customer's, or client's birthday or anniversary
- sincerely listening to the response when you ask someone, "How are you?"
- asking your administrative assistant if you can get him or her a cup of coffee
- leaving a larger-than-expected tip for the waitress who regularly serves you breakfast
- wishing someone a great day — and really meaning it
- helping a coworker fix a flat tire in the parking lot
- sharing your knowledge with someone in the office who needs help
- going out of your way to let coworkers know you appreciate something they did or said
- asking your coworkers meaningful questions about things that are important to them, then actively listening — really listening — to the response

I remember the first time I (Bill) walked into the medical practice Walt operated in Kissimmee, Florida. What I experienced took me by surprise — a smiling face. The receptionist stood up, beamed at me over the counter, and said, "Hi, how can I help you?" I was impressed! If your experience is anything like mine, you'll relate when I say I often feel more like a bother than a cared-for patient in many medical offices. Most of us have had the experience of being greeted by a glass window and a clipboard to sign in on. You can only hope that someone realizes you've arrived and will in time call your name.

Not so at Heritage Family Physicians, where a friendly person greeted me and others by name and with a smile. The staff was genuinely *delighted* that I was there, and there was no doubt that they were interested in helping me.

And that's not all. If the doctor was running late, one of the office personnel would alert patients of the approximate time the doctor would see them and then ask, "Is that OK?" This kind of behavior speaks volumes. It says that their patients are important to them and that patients' time is valuable. It shows that they care.

Ordinary? Yes. Powerful? Absolutely. Small, common courtesies such as these gave witness to their patients that something was different about their medical business, their staff members, and their doctors. They created a foundation of goodwill in which trusting relationships could develop, which resulted over time in many spiritual conversations with patients.

COMMON COURTESIES ARE DELIBERATE

Being known around the office in a general way as a nice person is a good thing. But we're talking about something more deliberate, namely, performing specific acts of kindness in ways that connect you positively and personally with another individual. By doing so, you lay a foundation for future spiritual influence.

Every encounter we have with another person ought to be coupled with a prayer: *Lord, show me how you want me to care for this person, and may this person see you in me.* Who knows what God may do? When the boy brought Jesus five loaves and two fish—pretty ordinary items *and* pretty meager—Jesus made an incredible feast (John 6:1–13). When we offer God our small, ordinary actions, deliberately putting them in his hands, amazing things can happen.

Darla had worked at her job for more than nineteen years. She was very good at what she did. If she had one complaint about her work, it was that she seldom felt appreciated. But that changed when Lea became her manager. The first week they worked together, Lea went out of her way to let Darla know when she had done a good job. At least once a day she relayed to Darla her appreciation for jobs well done.

As time passed, Lea would sometimes cut garden flowers and put them on Darla's desk. She sent her a card on her work anniversary. When she traveled, Lea would bring Darla small gifts. Lea would even brag about Darla at management meetings. As you can imagine, not only did Darla's enjoyment of work increase, but her work performance began to improve as well.

Darla began to trust Lea in a way she hadn't trusted any other manager she'd had. So when Darla and her husband began having problems with a teenage son, guess who she wanted to talk to? That's right—Lea. In Lea she found a sympathetic, compassionate listener, someone who really *heard* her. And when Lea offered a story of how a biblical principle had helped her family, Darla listened. *Really* listened.

COMMON COURTESIES ARE GENUINE

Kindness can't be faked—at least not consistently. Although common courtesies are deliberate, they are not manipulative or insincere. Even the kindest act performed insincerely will have an odd smell to it. Manipulation has a way of making itself known, and no one wants to be someone else's project. But caring about another person is not disconnected from a desire for that person to someday have a serious encounter with the God who cares more deeply about him or her than anyone else does.

Common courtesies are behaviors that are a natural but intentional overflow from a sincere heart in which the Spirit of God is at work. The kinds of behavior that build spiritual equity come from who you really are on the inside, not from religious duty or obligation. Paul talks about this in a letter to believers in Colossae: "So then, just as you received Christ Jesus as Lord, continue to live in him, rooted and built up in him, strengthened in the faith as you were taught, and overflowing with thankfulness" (Colossians 2:6–7).

One of the most enjoyable parts of being a person of spiritual influence is allowing your God-designed temperament and God-given gift(s) to overflow into your professional life in natural and comfortable, yet intentional, ways. Jesus emphasized this principle when he said, "For out of the overflow of the heart the mouth speaks. The good man brings good things out of the good stored up in him, and the evil man brings evil things out of the evil stored up in him" (Matthew 12:34–35).

It's consistency—small things repeated over time—that makes an impact and causes people to see Jesus in us. No matter how hostile a person may be to spiritual things, a Christlike character is overwhelmingly attractive. That's why when Paul talks about the fruit of the Spirit, he says, "Against such things there is no law" (Galatians 5:23).

COMMON COURTESIES CREATE OPPORTUNITIES

> If people know that you are a Christian, they are watching everything you are doing. A key part of integrity is not only trying to do the right thing, but also having the humility to admit when you mess up. That opens the door to authentic relationships. I think non-Christians are looking for authentic relationships. They can tell whether you have ulterior motives.
>
> *Jack Alexander, travel and hospitality industry*

Practice common courtesies consistently, and people will pay attention. Add in an excellent job performance, and people will pay attention to what you say as well as what you do. And if God is at work in their hearts, they'll want to get to know you better. Sometimes they'll even ask you questions, which will allow you to talk about how you've experienced Jesus in your life. In the chapters that follow, we'll talk about ways you can graciously foster curiosity through the answers you give. You don't have to worry about creating interest. That's God's job. Our job is to be interesting and to allow what Jesus is doing in our hearts to be seen by others.

COMMON COURTESIES TAKE TIME

The chief criticism we receive about the agrarian model of evangelism is that it's too slow. But the feedback we receive from the majority of Christians we've trained (now more than ten thousand persons) indicates that spending time on cultivation results in many more opportunities to plant and harvest in the workplace than are accomplished by aggressive methods of evangelism. Remember Jim? He tried to harvest in a corporation where he had done *no* cultivation, and look what happened (see pages 76–77).

Anyone involved in gardening knows that attempting to collect a harvest at the wrong time will result in unripe fruit. What's more, as any experienced gardener or farmer will tell you, you will not harvest anything without first working at cultivation and planting. Don't expect people to stop and ask you about Jesus the next time you do something nice. Be patient. Like monthly contributions to your retirement account, common courtesies can amount to something more over the course of time—including the opportunity to talk about deeper life issues.

Recently I (Bill) sat next to a young woman from Belgium on a flight across the Atlantic. I've never considered myself the poster child for gifted evangelism, so I had no illusions about leading this woman to Jesus between time zones. But I believed I could be part of the process. I felt an intense responsibility to jump in and see where God might lead this chance encounter. Because we were on a French airline, I took a chance and wished her *bon appétit* before a meal. This small courtesy—the first words spoken between us—led to a discussion in which I had opportunity to talk about basic spirituality. Toward the end of the flight I offered information I hoped she would find useful as she took up residence in the United States. I have a Christian friend in the car business in the city to which she's moving. Maybe they'll connect, and he'll extend her another common courtesy. Maybe at some point she'll wonder why so many people have taken an interest in her. But that's in God's hands.

> God put you here and you don't have to create opportunities to serve him. He is going to create divine appointments for you. The world is so full of human needs that they will evidence themselves in one way or another. We just need to be prepared to open our hand and say, "Here's what I have to offer. Are you willing to take it?" I had a chief financial officer walk into my office and say, "You got a minute?" He shut the door, sat down, and said, "There's something different about you. You just make decisions differently. Would you mind explaining that to me?"
>
> *Merrill Oster,*
> *business journalist*

COMMON COURTESIES DEMONSTRATE OUR BELIEFS

When we carry out common courtesies in the workplace (or when we do not), we demonstrate our core beliefs. The Bible clearly teaches that true love is love in action. In other words, common courtesies can be the most basic way we show love in action. The apostle John wrote, "Dear children, let us not love with words or tongue but with actions and in truth" (1 John 3:18).

Sincere love starts in our hearts but always plays itself out in our hands and feet—in what we do. Failure to love our coworkers through acts of kindness and courtesy actually communicates that we *don't* love them. It bears repeating: True love is love in action. But here's something else we must remember: Action—even common courtesies—without love is counterfeit. Paul wrote to the Corinthian church about this principle:

> If I speak in the tongues of men and of angels, but have not love, I am only a resounding gong or a clanging cymbal. If I have the gift of prophecy and can fathom all mysteries and all knowledge, and if I have a faith that can move mountains, but have not love, I am nothing. If I give all I possess to the poor and surrender my body to the flames, but have not love, I gain nothing.
>
> 1 Corinthians 13:1–3

We hope you see that being Jesus' witness is actually a simple proposition if we're experiencing God's grace. You don't need a theological education, and you don't need to know all the answers. It doesn't take great giftedness, but it does take determination to show the love of Jesus to people around you: "In the same way, let your light shine before men, that they may see your good deeds and praise your Father in heaven" (Matthew 5:16).

THE BOTTOM LINE

Being Jesus' witness in the workplace is simple and begins with common courtesies—not techniques and strategies to communicate the gospel message.

6

FOSTERING CURIOSITY

Jan was a successful thirty-five-year-old real estate agent who had worked in Sam's office for three years. The high-stress job had taken its toll on her physically, and one day she told Sam that her doctor had recommended exploratory day-surgery and that she'd be out of work for several days. Sam could sense her anxiety as she talked. He also knew that she had little spiritual background or interest.

Jan knew that Sam and several other coworkers were followers of Jesus, but she hadn't responded positively to any previous spiritual conversations. On at least one occasion she had expressed hostility toward several popular Christian leaders because of their stand on abortion. Sam, however, decided to seize the moment and relate a brief story of how he had found peace when he once faced a serious illness.

Jan rolled her eyes as she felt a sermon coming on, but she was drawn in by Sam's personal story. She listened intently. Sam concluded by saying, "Jan, God didn't heal me immediately, like I asked him to, but I found something more valuable. Through that experience, I developed a relationship with a God who wanted to walk through every problem with me, and that's made all the difference in the world. I'd love to tell you more sometime if you're interested."

Jan's eyes welled up with tears. "Maybe I need to know a God like that." Sam knew she had been touched and sensed that the spiritual door to her heart had opened a bit wider.

THE POWER OF PERSONAL NARRATIVE

Why do you think Jan responded so positively to a story when she failed to respond to other methods of communication? Well, if you've ever attended a well-scripted movie, you know the power of a story. Stories speak to the emotions first, often bypassing prejudices. Stories seize the imagination. They are one of the greatest resources we have in the cultivation stage with pre-Christians. Stories allow us to "reach out and touch someone."

When we try to communicate the facts of the gospel to people who haven't expressed an interest in what we believe, they generally have two strong impressions: (1) They feel we are being arrogant, as they hear us saying, *I know the truth and you don't*; and (2) they sense a condescending benevolence—"you're lost, you poor thing; let me help you." These impressions do not foster a desire in a person to know more. They can, in fact, raise emotional obstacles to further spiritual progress. If we haven't spent time cultivating, chances are pretty good that we'll only make the soil of their hearts harder.

To individuals with a predominantly modern mind-set, truth is scientific and universal. You can talk with them about evidence, proof, and logic—and they'll get what you're saying. But for many people in this postmodern era, truth is personal and experiential. Emotions are more important to decision making than facts. When you tell a personal story, you don't intend to proclaim that something is true for everyone—even though it may be. You're a witness who shares your personal experience, which then has the potential to resonate with someone else's longings. You connect on an emotional level. Without a doubt, the way we communicate our faith needs as much as ever to be informed by biblical understanding, solid thinking, and good evidence, but by starting with personal experience—entering the heart through the gate of emotion—we stand a much better chance of influencing the mind.

Taking the viewpoint of a postmodernist, Sarah Hinlicky tells us what she believes is the best way to communicate the gospel:

> So you're in quite a pickle: you can't tell us that the Church has "the Truth," and we know that the Church won't miraculously cure us of our misery. What do you have left to persuade us? One thing: the story. We are story people. We know narratives, not ideas. Our surrogate parents were the TV and the VCR, and we can spew out entertainment trivia at the drop of a hat. We treat our ennui with stories,

more and more stories, because they're the only things that make sense; when the external stories fail, we make a story of our own lives. You wonder why we're so self-destructive, but we're looking for the one story with staying power, the destruction and redemption of our own lives. That's to your advantage: you have the best redemption story on the market.1

Stories give a person an experiential view of the truth through the window of your life. It's not just philosophical; it is tangible and authentic. Because people remember stories, it gives listeners the opportunity to think at their own pace about what you've said rather than forcing an immediate intellectual showdown. Simply put, people want to see the truth *pictured* in our lives. That's why *faith flags* and *faith stories* are such powerful ways to communicate spiritual truth and create curiosity.

FAITH FLAGS

Faith flags are perhaps the simplest and least threatening way to introduce faith into any conversation. They provide the briefest glimpse of how faith is working in your life. Faith flags are brief statements—the bare nuggets of a story. They are told in the natural course of a conversation. They help you identify yourself as someone who is serious about faith. Faith flags are about identity. Just as a flag helps you recognize the nationality of a ship, faith flags help a person recognize you as someone to whom faith, the Bible, prayer, and God is important. Look at these examples:

- After your employee pays you a compliment about how great it is to work with you, you say: "We've been looking for someone like you. You're filling a huge void I prayed about for a long time."
- When someone does a great job, you say: "It seems to me that God has really gifted you in your ability to manage details."
- When someone opens up about an opportunity or a struggle, you say: "Boy, that's a tough situation. If it's OK with you, I would love to pray for you."

- In response to a positive comment about your ethical behavior, you say: "Although I don't always get it right, I'm trying to follow the principles the Bible teaches that appear to me to still be so effective for our business dealings—even today. That's important to me."
- On closing a great deal, you say: "Everyone worked really hard, but God surely blessed us on this one."
- In a conversation with someone who mentions that he is discouraged, you say: "I remember a time when I was more discouraged than I had ever been. A friend suggested I read some passages in the Bible, and it really helped me."
- In response to a positive comment about how you handled a difficult person, you say: "Thanks. I'm sure I would have lost it a year ago. I guess that means God is making at least a little progress in me."
- During a conversation about struggles with children, you say: "There've been plenty of times when we've been up against a wall with our kids, clueless about what to do. We read books and had long talks. But—and this may come as a surprise to you—some of the best help we found came from the Bible."
- During a conversation about marriage, you say: "I can't believe how much of a difference it's made in two stubborn people's lives to get in tune with the spiritual dimension of life."

GUIDELINES FOR RAISING FAITH FLAGS

If you want your faith flags to be effective, there are two very important principles to keep in mind. The first is this: *Faith flags must occur as a natural part of conversation.* They need to fit what's being said. They are not random messages that fly in from left field. They are intentional but not contrived—a simple expression of the reality of your faith at a given moment.

When John's company found out they had lost an important client to another firm, a gloomy atmosphere settled over the entire office. At the end of the day, Bob walked into John's office and slouched into a chair. They discussed what had happened, and then Bob said, "Man, this is so disappointing." After a pause he asked, "John, how do you handle stuff like this?"

John stared at the ceiling and said, "I guess when you've been in this business as long as I have, you learn to roll with the punches." He paused and decided to share a faith flag. "But you know, Bob, my faith has made a huge difference in how I look at these disappointments. This is where I'm supposed to be, win or lose." Bob was silent, taking it all in. Then John said, "Enough of this gloom! Let's go grab a bite to eat."

Here's the second principle: *Faith flags should take no longer than twenty seconds to share.* They are, at the most, a few sentences long—a simple comment, not a commentary. John's answer, for example, was short and to the point and flowed in as a natural part of the conversation. This faith flag let Bob know that John's faith was giving him some

> One of our corporate values is behaving with the highest sense of integrity. I have frequently asked, "Well, how do you define what is right and wrong?" and have used that as a way to say that I believe the Bible is the ultimate source of right and wrong. That has sometimes led to a meaningful discussion.
>
> *Marvin N. Schoenhals,
> financial services*

practical help in his business struggles. But John didn't assume that Bob was particularly interested in having a spiritual discussion at that moment. Bob wasn't asking for a deep theological explanation of pain and suffering. His question, though almost rhetorical in nature, did give John an opportunity to say something about his faith.

THINGS TO AVOID IN USING FAITH FLAGS

There are two things you'll want to avoid as you use faith flags. First, *take care not to identify yourself as a member of a particular church or denomination.* You're trying to identify yourself as someone to whom faith, prayer, the Bible, or God is important. Men and women who are bored with Baptists, miffed at Methodists, or peeved at Presbyterians will likely transfer to you any ill feelings they may be harboring if you announce your church affiliation before they're attracted to something in you personally. We're not saying you should hide your church affiliation, but keep in mind that identifying yourself as a member of a particular denomination at this stage may present an obstacle.

Second, *avoid pointing to your faith as a reason for not doing something*. We'll talk more about this later, but since Christianity is not a list of regulations, we want to be careful not to give people the impression we're merely talking about religious rules. Unlike any other world religion, Christianity is a personal relationship with God through his Son Jesus. Statements such as "I don't drink [or dance or smoke or ...] because it's against my religion" do not create curiosity. What you're declaring may be true in your life, but it rarely will build a bridge of interest and trust. If your friends believe that Christianity is only a list of do's and don'ts, you've only succeeded in further hardening already hard ground. They might identify you as a person of faith, but your faith flag runs the risk of creating more condemnation than curiosity. This kind of communication almost always sounds judgmental to a non-Christian.

THE RESULTS

Raising faith flags helps you see and evaluate what God is doing in someone's life. A faith flag looks for, but doesn't demand, a response. When you raise a faith flag, you'll be able to watch for the person's verbal and nonverbal responses and gauge interest in a nonthreatening way.

When we run up a faith flag, we watch to see if anyone salutes. For example, Bob's silence after listening to John sent John a powerful message: Drop the subject for now! There's one thing every wise farmer knows: It's unproductive to plant in uncultivated ground. God's Spirit needed to soften the soil of Bob's heart a little more.

An essential element of expressing grace in the workplace is discovering what God is doing in the lives of your friends and colleagues, and then joining him there. Perhaps more than any other tool, faith flags give us the ability each day to ask intentionally about each encounter, "What is God doing?" and "What would he have me do in response?" If God is at work to draw a person to himself, eventually this person is going to respond to faith flags, even though it may not happen immediately.

In the end, a faith flag creates an opportunity. When God is at work in a person, he or she usually wants to know more. According to 1 Peter 3:15, the act of someone *asking* is the trigger that creates an opportunity to take a conversation deeper spiritually. If God is creating a spiritual hunger in a person, we can count on this: Someone who is hungry will ask. Then we'll have the opportunity to say more—at the person's invitation.

FAITH STORIES

Just watch others the next time you're in the lunchroom or break room. People are telling stories. It's the way we communicate and connect with one another. *Faith stories* are the next communication step beyond faith flags. A faith story portrays in narrative form how God or a biblical principle became real to you. It is a testimony about a specific time when something spiritual happened to you. It doesn't tell someone how to know God, but it communicates that he is at work and making a meaningful difference in your life. God often uses these faith stories to intensify a hunger for him. It is a powerful way to communicate spiritual truth in an inviting form—especially in the workplace.

GUIDELINES FOR TELLING FAITH STORIES

Here are a few guidelines for relating stories from your own spiritual life:

- Faith stories should be a natural part of the conversation. They are not contrived or planned with respect to what will be said.
- Faith stories are not faith sermons, so they generally shouldn't take more than a minute or two to tell. Limit the subject of the story to God, the Bible, or prayer. Bringing up specific churches, denominations, or religious leaders puts us at risk of being identified with a person or group that may cause a barrier for the person.

Faith stories provide a glimpse of what it is like to be God's child. We hope non-Christian colleagues already sense something attractive about you. Faith stories explain *why* there's something attractive. They're a glimpse of the faith that is at work in you. When you tell a story that corresponds with a need in their lives, your story will resonate with them. For example, to go to God in prayer — to know that he personally hears us and cares about what's hurting us — is an awesome privilege of a child of God. I (Walt) often told this faith story to patients facing some medical difficulty:

> I know something of what you must be feeling. When my daughter Kate was eleven, she had a life-threatening grand mal seizure. We rushed her to the hospital, where it took our family doctor over an hour to stop the seizure. By this time she had stopped breathing and had to be put on a ventilator. In the ICU the doctors told us her brain wave was flat — they weren't sure if the medicines or brain death had caused it. All night Barb and I stayed by her bedside. We hugged, and we cried. We were in total shock. Then a friend came by. He didn't have a lot of advice or fancy words. He just showed us how to pray. That night spent in prayer began a practice that God has used in our lives ever since.

For a number of persons who felt helpless, this faith story opened the door to many conversations about prayer, the Bible, and God. It was an entry point for me (Walt) to explain to patients who showed interest that God not only loves us enough to listen but that he loves us enough to have sent his only Son to die for us when we were absolutely helpless.

EXAMPLES OF FAITH STORIES

The following samples may give you insight into how to fit the story to the situation.

When someone affirms you for doing a job well: "Thanks for noticing. I really don't think I'm much different from other people around here, except that about two years ago I found out I have another boss whom I really want to please. To my surprise I discovered that the Bible teaches that God cares about the work I do. Not only does the person who signs my check deserve good work, but God deserves my very best as well. Your comment means I must be making progress. Thanks."

In a conversation about business decisions: "Strange as it may seem, a lot of the decisions I make are based on principles from the Bible. A few years ago a friend showed me some business principles in the Bible. He said that these principles could help a business run well. I was floored to find so much practical information in such an old book. If you're interested, I'd be glad to have lunch together someday and share with you what I've learned."

When a difficult decision has to be made: "I don't like to parade my faith around here, but I spend a lot of time praying about decisions like this. I discovered a few years ago that God really cares about my work. He doesn't promise to make me a billionaire, but I figured I was missing out big-time if I didn't talk things over with my Creator and seek his guidance. No one knows me or this business better than he does. I've found that he loves me and cares about what I do—what we do here at this company. It's made a major difference in my attitude, and I think it gives me an advantage. I know I'm a different person; and best of all, I can sleep at night."

In response to a comment about your calm in the midst of a storm: "It hasn't always been this way. I had high anxiety down to a science at the beginning of my career. My mentor at the time noticed that it was affecting my work and asked me, 'What's your exit strategy?' It took me a minute to figure out he wasn't talking about investments but life. He explained to me that his exit strategy was based on a personal relationship with God. That was the secret of true peace. If you ever want to know more about this, let me know."

> I frequently bring into the story my grandmother, because she taught me so many things. It's not like me preaching. I say, "You mind if I tell you a story about my grandma?" Grandma was one of the original corporates. She was chief executive officer of the kitchen. She would pass out a cookie and talk about Christ all in the same sentence, without changing the tone of voice. It was that example of not having a Sunday and a Monday mind that made it easy for me to naturally move the conversation back and forth to spiritual subjects.
>
> *Merrill Oster,*
> *business journalist*

In a conversation about a lost business opportunity: "In 1997 I had a deal go south and it about killed me. I had worked on it for months and put everything else on hold. I was bitter toward this guy who didn't keep his word, and I didn't think I could pull out financially. The bank was calling, I couldn't sleep at night, and I was having chest pains. I had no other option but to trust God with my business. I realized I needed to work smart and do my best work, but in the end, God really controls the results. If I screw up or do something stupid, well, I deserve to lose a deal. But if I've done my best and it still doesn't go down, then I know there's a reason. You know me—I don't like to lose, but I can't tell you how much peace it brings me to know that God's running the show."

DEVELOPING YOUR OWN FAITH STORIES

Here are some guidelines to help you surface your own faith stories:

Step 1: Make a list of times when you had a meaningful encounter with God. It may have been a time:

- when God did something meaningful or significant in your life
- when you enjoyed and experienced pleasure in your relationship with God
- when you experienced intimacy or renewal in your relationship with God
- when God spoke clearly to you or gave you guidance
- when God worked through you to accomplish his purposes

Step 2: Choose one or two of these experiences and write a brief faith story about each.

DO'S AND DON'TS FOR STIMULATING CURIOSITY

Through the years we've learned several important principles pertaining to raising faith flags and telling faith stories:

TRUST THE HOLY SPIRIT TO DO HIS WORK IN HIS TIMING

Don't give in to the temptation to play Holy Spirit. Simply tell your story and watch for a response. Resist attempts to convict, but let the power of what God did for you and in you settle into the hearer's heart. Don't try to moralize or dress up the principle you want the person to get. Make sure your story is sincere, and let the Holy Spirit do his job.

A relationship with God is not a group decision. If we allow our self-worth to be wrapped up in someone's response, our behavior may become manipulative and our faith may repel an intelligent person. Pushing for a response is a declaration that we can't or won't trust God to do what is his work, and his alone, namely, salvation. As witnesses we can assist, but as much as we may want to, no one can take a step toward God for someone else. What we can do is talk about our personal relationship with God and how he has made a difference in our lives. Then we give control over to God.

A few years ago, I (Bill) became convicted that I had never explained the gospel to a friend. I had spent a lot of time with him and raised a lot of faith flags over the years, but he never seemed to get to the point of openness to the gospel message. Feeling guilty, I set up a lunch appointment. As we ate, I tried to make up for lost time, reaching for every spiritually stimulating thought and question I could find—short of spiritually clubbing him over the head. He ignored every opportunity I gave him to ask me more and turn the conversation to spiritual issues.

Thankfully he wasn't offended by my antics, but as we drove back to his office, I was frustrated, mad at myself, and mad at God. Then, out of the blue, my friend asked, "Bill, we've been studying

> There are people God is drawing, so my prayer is that God would bring me together with them in his timing. I am also proactive in this by saying something spiritual in the conversation that the other person can pick up on. If they pick up on it, I'll go as far as they are willing to talk. If you say something and they don't respond, that time is probably not the best to go on with it. Early on, I offended people by going on when they didn't want to hear it.
>
> *Norm Miller,*
> *automotive supply*

the gospel of John in my Sunday school class, and I'm confused about this *born again* thing. What does that mean?"

I was stunned. After I collected myself, I gave him a short answer that didn't seem to satisfy him. Meanwhile we had pulled into the parking lot at his office and he needed to get back to work, so I offered to meet with him in a few days to discuss his questions. He jumped at the chance.

REGULATE THE DOSAGE

Avoid the temptation of unloading the spiritual dump truck on people as soon as they express even a pinch of spiritual interest. People need time to think about what we say. Give them space. Even if they ask further questions, be careful not to overload them. The idea is to stimulate curiosity and keep a person asking for more. Notice that John's faith flag (page 91) gave a minimum of information: "My faith has made a huge difference in how I look at these disappointments." He didn't answer who, how, or why. He just laid out the bare facts to stimulate Bob's curiosity. Keeping things short and sweet avoids the danger of running so far ahead of a person you run the risk of losing the listener.

BE HONEST AND AUTHENTIC

Don't be afraid of showing your flaws. Faith in Jesus doesn't solve all of life's problems or make any of us perfect. There is a victorious aspect to the Christian faith, but a lot of life involves failure and heartbreak. When we cover up our frailty and only talk about how wonderful life is, we reveal a lack of solid understanding of grace and what God has done for us. We have nothing to lose by being authentic, because we're forgiven and accepted by God. We also fail to see that non-Christians are not attracted by our victories but by God's grace. They need to see the process (where we've come from), not just the product (what we are today). If we sanitize our story and eliminate our struggles, non-Christians won't be able to identify with us, and they'll think—rightly so—that we are phony!

The benevolent superiority we sometimes express toward non-Christians is a major turnoff. Yes, God has changed us. But that's exactly the point. Though we would never come right out and say it, we may act as though *we* changed ourselves and are now vastly different from our colleagues. Could this be why some non-Christians seem almost gleeful when Christians, especially those in the public eye, fail? "See, they really weren't any different from the rest of us!" they may crow. Well, whoever said we were? We all struggle with sinful drives, desires, and dilemmas. As Christians we still fail; we still use bad judgment at times. There are, of course, things that *are* different about us, but that's *God's* doing, not ours. This fact ought to make us the humblest people on earth.

But beware: attributing *everything* to God often sounds like false humility to a non-Christian. For example, responding to a compliment with "No, it wasn't me. It was God" may be understood by a non-Christian as "If you had *any* spiritual insight at all, which, of course, I have a considerable amount of, you would understand that it wasn't me; it was God." This sounds incredibly disingenuous — humble words with an arrogant underpinning. Many times patients and their family members will praise a physician after recovery from illness. A number of doctors we know first express sincere personal thanks and then go on to raise a faith flag: "You know, there's really only so much a doctor can do. I treat — to the best of my ability — but God is the one who heals."

SPEAK THEIR LANGUAGE

Is it possible that we're telling the world's greatest story in a "foreign" language? One of the most difficult things to do is to free our communication of insider language that only Christians understand nowadays. Casual conversation with non-Christians is not the only problem, however. Even professionally written books, tracts, and popular evangelistic tools are often full of words and concepts that many people find confusing and at times even offensive. To the uninitiated, listening to Christian television can sometimes seem like listening to a foreign-language station.

Here are a few of the obstacles Christians need to overcome with regard to speaking in a way that will communicate to their hearers today.

Some Words and Terms Are Confusing

Every group has special terminology. Whether we're talking techno-speak, medical lingo, legalese, or Christian theology, certain words make no sense to outsiders—even interested outsiders. Here are some typical phrases we ask nonbelievers to understand and respond to: to be washed in the blood, to be redeemed, to ask Jesus into your heart, to be saved, to be justified, to repent of your transgressions and iniquities, to be born again, to receive the gospel message.

In days gone by, Americans were more theologically and biblically literate, but today we can't assume that people understand the terms we often use in Christian circles. As you seek to communicate with non-Christians, you would do well to come up with other words to convey the meaning behind these concepts.

Some Words Have Become Offensive

For various reasons, certain words may become offensive to non-Christians. Take the word *lost*, for example. In the parables of Jesus in Luke 15, Luke uses the word to describe people who are separated from God. There's no doubt it's a biblical concept. But many non-Christians do not appreciate being labeled as *lost*. They perceive it as a derogatory comment about their lack of intelligence or their inability to get their life together rather than as a description of their spiritual separation from God.

Born again is another perfectly good biblical term that sadly has begun to raise red flags when we use it in conversations with some non-Christians. A *born-again* Christian has been wrongly defined in some people's minds to mean a narrow-minded, conservative, politically right-wing person. If you tell people they need to be born again, they may think you're trying to get them to join the "religious right" rather than inviting them to experience new life in Jesus.

Some Words Have Become Misleading

If culture has redefined a biblical term, we would be wise to exercise care in how we use it so we don't create confusion. Take the word *sin*, for example. Fifty years ago, most Americans understood sin to be behavior that was essentially bad in and of itself. Today sin is often seen as a behavior on an arbitrary list made up by some person or some group, infringing on your freedom to seek pleasure and pursue happiness your own way. Though neither definition hits the mark biblically, sin was at one time considered something that good people tried to avoid doing. When they did sin, they felt guilty. Somehow they knew sinners needed forgiveness—even if they didn't understand it fully. So when people understood that "all have sinned" (Romans 3:23), they knew *all* needed to be forgiven by God. Today sin is viewed by some as a "thou shalt not" rule they need to be freed from, not forgiven for. As we consider our audience, then, we may communicate more clearly when we use a term such as *wrongdoing*. All of us can agree that we've done wrong things—things we wish we could do over.

When we (the Peels) lived in Nashville, we were privileged to get to know the members of the popular Christian singing group Jars of Clay, which takes its name from 2 Corinthians 4:7—"we have this treasure in jars of clay." Even though these artists often sing about faith, they captured the imagination of non-Christians, receiving positive reviews from publications such as *Entertainment Weekly*, *Rolling Stone*, and *Spin*. Their appeal has to do with the quality of their music, as well as their authenticity and the way they express their faith in their songs. One writer said, "Most intriguing is Jars' winsome way of expressing their faith without clichés or inside-the-Bible-beltway lingo." According to Jars of Clay lead singer Dan Haseltine, "The topics we deal with are universal in so many ways. And we're not only singing to Christians, so why would I want to write a song that uses all this language that only Christians would understand?"[2]

CURIOSITY RAISED THE DEAD

Curiosity may have killed the cat, but it's an important characteristic of a person's journey to new life in Jesus Christ. Faith flags and faith stories are effective ways to cultivate this curiosity, for Christians to back the testimony of their lives (their competence, character, and concern) with the testimony of their lips (communi-cation). Curiosity stimulates dialogue and the possibility of further communication, which softens hard-hearted resistance and leads to understanding.

THE BOTTOM LINE										
Less is usually more in your speech. Learn to say less about your faith and accomplish more by using stories told in a language that's winsome and understandable.										

BUILDING STRATEGIC
ALLIANCES

If you are like most Christians in the workplace, time is at a premium. Jim was a stockbroker with an aggressive firm that had rigorous performance quotas. After two years he had developed a solid client base. In fact, he was recognized as a star performer. Jim, however, was haunted by his inability to integrate his faith into his work world. He had numerous open doors—not only with clients but with coworkers as well—to bring up spiritual issues. But the thought of getting into a deep, prolonged conversation about Jesus just as the stock market was closing kept him silent.

The limitations of time aside, none of us—working alone—can be the spiritually influential person for Christ we were meant to be. Not long ago a man came to me (Bill) toward the end of the day, wanting to discuss his career frustrations. The conversation became fairly intense, but I eventually realized I wasn't going to be able to help him—even though he wanted help and I wanted to help him. It was going to take more time and a different set of gifts and abilities from mine. I needed a teammate. In fact, everyone who is attempting to share Christ in the workplace needs teammates.

THE TEAMWORK TREND

The competitive pressures of today's workplace are forcing people to recognize the limitations of working alone. Increasingly, individuals are working in teams. Even in our schools and colleges, young people are being taught to work in teams.

The teamwork trend has hit the corporate world in dramatic fashion. Companies of all sizes are teaming up with other companies in strategic alliances to enhance their competitiveness in the marketplace and keep pace with the rapid changes of technological innovation. Today, strategic alliances are sweeping through nearly every sector of commerce, as companies team up to create imaginative strategies to enhance brand identity, connect with customers, and attract top-notch employees. It's not just that alliances are surging, says leadership expert Peter Drucker, but a "worldwide restructuring" is occurring in the shape of alliances and partnerships.

Studies by the global management and technology consulting firm Booz, Allen & Hamilton reveal that the number of alliances in the United States has grown by 25 percent each year since 1987. And more than 20,000 corporate alliances were formed worldwide in a two-year period (2000-2001).[1]

Strategic alliances may be the hot new business trend, but the concept is not new. In fact, it's biblical, for the Bible tells us that we need one another. One company or one person can't do it all. God certainly didn't intend for one person to do it all. As it turns out, the apostle Paul would have made a great business consultant. The concept of the body of Christ, which Paul introduces us to in his letters (see especially 1 Corinthians 12:12–31; Ephesians 4:9–16), is God's universal rule for getting things done—true in commerce, true in family, true in church work, and true in evangelism.

Teams are God's universal rule. When he created Adam, God said, "It is not good for the man to be alone. I will make a helper suitable for him" (Genesis 2:18). So he made Eve. It took both of them together to reflect the image of God. The Hebrew word translated as "alone" in this verse carries an overtone of separation and even alienation, a sense of being incomplete—even the inability to perform well and to be complete. The Hebrew mind-set saw that humans truly live only insofar as they are related within their environment to partners with whom they share life and love, with whom they co-serve God, family, and community. Ultimately God himself is a team of three persons, each bringing a unique contribution to the work of the one God. God loves teams—he invented them, he designed them, he designed us to work in them!

Unlike the evangelistic models that focus on the *event* of sharing the gospel, the biblical *process* of evangelism requires a team. It is crucial to intentionally involve others as we seek to influence the workplace spiritually. It's important not only because of the unique gifts others bring to the process but also in the event a non-Christian's spiritual curiosity peaks when time-sensitive workplace issues and deadlines limit your own availability.

Remember Jim's concern about being caught in a conversation about Jesus as the market was closing? In this chapter we'll explore the importance of participating in a "strategic spiritual alliance" to alleviate time dilemmas and broaden your impact. We'll give concrete suggestions on how to create, assemble, and train a team to work together for spiritual influence. These principles are applicable for a Christian whose work setting is occupied predominantly by non-Christians as well as for a Christian who works in an office of fellow believers.

As we created "The Saline Solution" for health care professionals, we learned that doctors struggled with talking to patients about faith issues largely because of jam-packed schedules. What is a doctor to do, for example, if she is running an hour behind when a patient finally responds to the faith flags the doctor has raised in the past and wants to talk about what it means to trust Jesus? If she chooses to stay and talk to her patient, she gets further behind, and her staff and the patients sitting in the waiting room get angrier. If she doesn't respond, she feels guilty about walking away. This dilemma paralyzed most doctors until we were able to apply a principle out of their own culture to help them understand how they could treat the soul as well as the body in a busy practice.

When my partner, John Hartman, and I (Walt) came up against this dilemma, we realized we could apply a strategy already being used in our medical practice. We had created a "consult network," which we could tap into for referring a patient to another physician when that patient's physical or emotional needs were beyond our training. Just the same, we decided we could create a "spiritual consult team" to tap into for referring patients with spiritual needs we couldn't handle at the time. One of my mentors, noted hand surgeon Dr. Paul Brand, had introduced this idea to me. Dr. Brand put it this way:

> Even in an active practice of our profession, we need to know and have available to us (on call, as it were) other people who can participate with us in this great work of witnessing to the love of God. I believe we

should know people in our church and in our hospital—nurses, mothers, people who have been bereaved, people who have suffered, people who know how to sympathize and comfort—so that in our busyness, when we cannot give as much time as we ought to give, we can call on someone else to help. It would be wise to have a list of other members of the body of Christ who could help us in this great work.[2]

If you happen to be in a job with an impossible schedule, teamwork enables you to reach out to friends, colleagues, and customers without forcing you to add additional projects or tasks to an already crowded calendar. For most busy people, it's a matter of recognizing the opportunities we already have in our daily contacts. It's also a matter, as Dr. Brand suggests, of developing a team to work with us in living out our mutual concern for people who don't know Jesus—because we *cannot* do it alone.

If the busyness of your schedule hasn't suggested this to you already, you can be assured that it will. Teamwork is not only practical, as Dr. Brand reminds us, but it is essential—it's the way God designed our world to work.

THE IMPORTANCE OF A TEAM

As we reflect on the importance of a team, several crucial principles emerge from Scripture.

PRINCIPLE 1: NO ONE CAN DO IT ALL

What's true in business is also true spiritually. No one has what it takes to do everything we need to do, much less everything we want to do. We're limited by time—just twenty-four hours a day. We're limited by space—one place at a time. We're limited by abilities—no one has all the gifts.

If we insist on trying to do it all, not only will we burn out, we will end up offending God. Any time we feel overworked, we should consider whether we're thinking too highly of ourselves, taking on commitments God never intended us to tackle alone. The apostle Paul taught this clearly:

For by the grace given me I say to every one of you: Do not think of yourself more highly than you ought, but rather think of yourself with sober judgment, in accordance with the measure of faith God has given you. Just as each of us has one body with many members, and these members do not all have the same function, so in Christ we who are many form one body, and each member belongs to all the others. We have different gifts, according to the grace given us. If a man's gift is prophesying, let him use it in proportion to his faith. If it is serving, let him serve; if it is teaching, let him teach; if it is encouraging, let him encourage; if it is contributing to the needs of others, let him give generously; if it is leadership, let him govern diligently; if it is showing mercy, let him do it cheerfully.

Romans 12:3–8

There is only so much time and energy to go around. When we say "yes" to someone, we are saying "no" to certain other opportunities with clients, customers, coworkers, friends, family, or our own personal needs. We need to be judicious about how we invest ourselves—and we must realize that we need others.

PRINCIPLE 2: YOU ARE CREATED TO WORK IN TANDEM WITH OTHERS

God wants others to join us in our work. There are other people who can handle some things better than we can because they've been gifted in ways that differ from the ways in which we've been gifted. When we're able to combine what we're good at with what others are good at, great things can happen. The Bible consistently teaches us to work as a body does, each part making its unique contribution. In the earliest days of the church, working together as a team was one of the reasons for its incredibly powerful impact.[3]

When we think back on how we came to believe in Jesus, most of us remember a specific person who led us into this relationship. For me (Bill) it was a staff member of Campus Crusade for Christ. Yet it really isn't the whole story. One of my early mentors told me that a number of people (anywhere from nine to sixteen) usually participate in a person's spiritual journey to Jesus. As I thought back, I identified thirteen people God used to help me make mini-decisions toward faith: my parents (1, 2), my senior high Sunday school teacher (3), a high school girlfriend (4) who took me to her church where I heard her pastor (5) preach the gospel, a couple of awesome sophomore advisers at Southern Methodist University (6, 7) who held a Bible study every Sunday night that a high school friend (9) on my freshman dorm floor dragged me to, several national traveling speakers (10, 11, 12) who presented the gospel in a large group setting, and a seminary student on Crusade staff who hung out on my dorm floor (13).

For me (Walt), it also was a staff member of Campus Crusade for Christ, Rich McGee. Rich was there at the harvest, but here, too, Rich isn't the whole story. God used many others to help me make mini-decisions toward faith: my parents (1, 2), my aunt Martha (3), my grandmother (4), two Episcopal priests (5, 6), a small group at a summer church camp (7–12), a high school girlfriend (13) whom I watched grow in her faith, a good friend on my high school football team (14), a campus pastor (15) and members of his church (16–22), a national traveling speaker (23) who presented the gospel in a large group setting, and three Louisiana State University football players (24–26) and a Crusade staff member (27) who hung around my dorm. Just recently I read the memoirs of a relative (28) who was praying for the generations to follow him.

Each of these individuals played an important role in our spiritual journeys. Although most didn't see us cross the line of faith, each helped us take a further step toward Jesus.

PRINCIPLE 3: YOU ARE NOT RESPONSIBLE TO MEET EVERY SPIRITUAL NEED YOU ENCOUNTER

A young woman came to see me (Bill), indignant that she had been fired for witnessing on the job. At first it sounded as though she had been discriminated against. Then I heard her story. Not only did she try to start a Bible study on company time, but also by witnessing and praying with her coworkers, she had consistently neglected her work as she tried to meet the spiritual needs she perceived in her coworkers. After a third reprimand, her boss made the decision to let her go. When I suggested that what she had done wasn't right, she told me she had to please God rather than men.

We've said this before, but it bears repeating: Christians in the marketplace have to be careful to give their employers their due — good work. It is possible to get so overextended in meeting spiritual needs that we neglect our work. If meeting a spiritual need causes you to neglect your work, think hard about whether someone else should meet this need.

PRINCIPLE 4: COUNT ON OTHERS WHEN YOU DON'T HAVE THE TIME, ENERGY, OR GIFTS TO MEET NEEDS

Don't feel you need to respond to every opportunity. God has called others to help meet needs, too, and if we have other work to do, we must be able to call on others to cover for us.

Even if you think you're the only Christian in your business, don't hesitate to look for a team. Other followers of Jesus will undoubtedly be around you somewhere — if not in your company, maybe it'll be a customer, supplier, or colleague in another business. Talk to your pastor and ask for help in finding other Christians with whom you can team up.

> It's important to realize that God is sovereign and that he not only calls you, but he puts you under authority. In my case, I have worked the last nineteen years for an organization that is not a Christian organization, but I have been amazed that as I have submitted to and sought to honor that authority, God has blessed the efforts.
>
> *Jack Alexander, travel and hospitality industry*

PRINCIPLE 5: THERE IS POWER AND ENCOURAGEMENT IN NUMBERS

The wise King Solomon said it pretty well. Though this Scripture is often read at weddings, the principle is universal:

Two are better than one,
   because they have a good return for their work:
If one falls down,

his friend can help him up.
But pity the man who falls
and has no one to help him up!
Also, if two lie down together, they will keep warm.
But how can one keep warm alone?
Though one may be overpowered,
two can defend themselves.
A cord of three strands is not quickly broken.

Ecclesiastes 4:9–12

PRINCIPLE 6: TEAMWORK WAS IMPORTANT TO JESUS AND THE EARLY CHURCH

The only time the Bible explicitly records that Jesus spent a whole night in prayer (other than perhaps at Gethsemane) was when he selected his team: "One of those days Jesus went out to a mountainside to pray, and spent the night praying to God. When morning came, he called his disciples to him and chose twelve of them, whom he also designated apostles" (Luke 6:12–13). This doesn't mean, of course, that this was the only time Jesus spent the night in prayer, but its singular mention certainly lends emphasis to how important the concept of team was to his ministry. And if Jesus chose to work with a team, delegating important responsibilities, we surely should consider how important a team is to our work as well.

Jesus passed the pattern of teamwork on to his disciples as well. When he sent them out to preach and heal, he sent them two by two: "Calling the Twelve to him, he sent them out two by two and gave them authority over evil spirits" (Mark 6:7). So it was for the early church, which consistently used Jesus' teamwork pattern when it sent out missionaries.[4] Interestingly, there is *not one* example in the Bible of a church led by a single pastor or elder. Anytime we see the establishment of a new church, we see the apostles appointing a team—a plurality of leaders.

Get the picture? How did we ever get the idea that an individual could lead a person to Jesus in isolation from the rest of the body of Christ? It's not only a mystery to us, but it's also a critical strategic error. Ministry always takes a team. If you want to have a spiritual impact on the men and women in your workplace, it will take a team.

DEVELOPING YOUR PERSONAL STRATEGIC ALLIANCE

Consider the following suggestions that can help you collaborate with others in ways that will maximize your spiritual impact.

ALLY WITH COWORKERS

Meet before work regularly to encourage each other and exchange ideas. It can be as simple as meeting to pray for your workplace and the non-Christians God lays on your heart. It doesn't matter if there are just two of you. That's enough, according to Jesus: "If two of you on earth agree about anything you ask for, it will be done for you by my Father in heaven. For where two or three come together in my name, there am I with them" (Matthew 18:19–20).

When John Hartman and I (Walt) opened a family medical practice, we found we could encourage, equip, and enable each other's ministry. Soon we were able to include our nurses and office staff in our workplace ministry.

ALLY WITH SUPPLIERS

Look for Christians within your company's strategic alliances. Enlist them to join you in prayer. Talk to them about who God is laying on your heart and about some ways both of you can help each person take steps toward Jesus.

Al owns a company that manufactures and distributes private-label cleaning products. Every time Al visits a company in Arkansas, the buyer sets up lunch with someone he wants Al to meet. Sometimes the conversation moves to spiritual topics and sometimes it doesn't, but the buyer and supplier always pray together for individuals in the company to come to Jesus.

ALLY WITH WELL-KNOWN LEADERS

When considering strategic partners, businesses benefit from alliances that add value and prestige. The same is true for individuals.

Who are the leaders in your field? Are any of them devoted followers of Jesus? If so, seek them out for their wisdom, but also look for opportunities to expose your colleagues, associates, or customers to them in nonthreatening settings. Your association with a well-recognized name can generate immediate credibility for you, which can then be translated into spiritual influence.

ALLY WITH COLLEAGUES FROM OTHER COMPANIES

I (Bill) meet once a month with several men and women in the real estate business in Dallas. We encourage each other and share wisdom and insight about good business strategies, but also about how to care for people personally and spiritually.

After the terrorist attacks of September 11, 2001, the real estate market in Dallas went flat, and a number of companies began to downsize. So the first topic we discussed that fall was how a Christian would go about downsizing a company. As followers of Jesus, these men and women were concerned about how the handling of a downsizing would reflect on Jesus to nonbelievers. They knew that the relationships Christians had been cultivating with non-Christians were at stake.

As they pooled their wisdom, they agreed that it was legitimate for a company in serious jeopardy to implement downsizing. Failing to save the company and preserve as many jobs as possible could be worse than enduring the disappointment or anger of a few employees. They also urged that the whole process be bathed in a great deal of prayer about each decision, as well as a commitment to treat each person with dignity and to be as generous as possible to departing employees.

While not all the stories are in as of this writing, the difficult situation of implementing downsizing turned into a positive experience for several of these employers. Their compassion toward their employees opened doors for spiritual conversation. Had these employers not sat down with each other for encouragement and sharing of wisdom, things might not have gone as well.

ALLY WITH A CUSTOMER OR CLIENT

Customers can be one of the richest sources of team members. Obviously, some customer relationships are extremely short-lived, but if you have return customers or enjoy an extended relationship with clients, these folks can be an important partner in your spiritual strategic alliances. You can connect a client with a Christian who has dealt with a similar business problem, for example, and not only help a client but also make a connection for Jesus.

In my (Walt's) business, my partner, John, and I felt comfortable hiring nonbelievers. We were, quite simply, looking for the most competent and qualified individuals—both personally and professionally—for the particular jobs we had to fill. During our interviews with nonbelievers, we were honest about our spiritual goals and visions. We didn't ask them to agree with these, but wanted to be sure they were comfortable working for such a company.

Our Christian patients (clients) always seemed to enjoy coming to a practice where professional competence was job one. But they would also notice a subtle difference between employees who were believers and those who were not. So on occasion I would ask patients to join me in praying for our employees who didn't yet know the Lord. Our customers became members of our spiritual team.

Over my sixteen years in that medical practice, at least five employees have come to trust Jesus as their Savior and Lord. What a privilege! Yet I'm convinced it was accomplished by the effort of a team that included our customers.

ALLY WITH A SERVICE PROVIDER

If you are in a position to refer your customers or clients to other service providers—attorneys, accountants, insurance agents, financial advisers, other manufacturers—making a referral to someone who is a follower of Jesus can bring in an additional positive Christian influence.

Yet when you make such a referral, you put your reputation on the line—and in someone else's hands. It's wise for you to take time to get to know a person or company and the quality of their work before you make a referral. Just because someone attends church or talks about Jesus doesn't mean he or she is serious about following Jesus in the workplace.

Keep in mind that things can happen beyond anyone's control, and we all make mistakes. Referrals don't always work out. Sometimes trust between two good people erodes for reasons that escape us. As you calculate the risk, however, remember that Jesus took an incredible risk in entrusting the gospel to us. Who among us would have put all our hopes into the ragtag group of disciples Jesus selected to carry his message? For that matter, why should he trust any of us to be on his team? We're all flawed. But he does trust us, and we must follow his lead as we trust others to do their part for God's kingdom.

ALLY WITH PASTORS

Your pastor can be one of your most important team members. Your pastor can personally provide assistance or network with other pastors and Christian counselors if someone you talk with needs professional help. Pastors can connect you with a variety of men and women with gifts and experiences important to your team. For example, if a colleague develops cancer, your pastor may be able to put you in touch with someone who has had a similar diagnosis. You in turn can gain insight from this person or possibly arrange a meeting with this person and your colleague.

After attending "The Saline Solution" conference with several doctors from his church, one pastor put together a team of Christians interested in having a spiritual impact in their workplace. Here's what he committed to do for them:

- He met with them each Friday to pray for opportunities to raise faith flags.
- He regularly asked them about opportunities they'd had to share their faith.
- He regularly visited them in their workplace.
- He connected them with other Christians when they were looking to hire new employees.
- He provided spiritual counsel upon request.

If you haven't done so already, take your pastor out to lunch and challenge him or her to join your strategic alliance.

ALLY WITH COMMUNITY SERVICE ORGANIZATIONS

Consider encouraging your business to engage in community service projects, joining forces with community organizations such as local shelters or with national organizations such as Habitat for Humanity. Imagine the opportunities for being a witness as you spend an evening a month at a community shelter or a weekend building a house with some of your coworkers.

ALLY WITH LOCAL WORKPLACE MINISTRIES

Some major cities have ministries that focus on the workplace, although there are not many of them yet. Here are some of the ministries we've heard about:

- Young Business Leaders of Birmingham, Alabama (ybl.org)
- Needle's Eye Ministries in Richmond, Virginia (needleseye.org)
- NAEN (National Affinity Evangelism Network) Ministries in Fremont, California—Silicon Valley (naenministry.org)

ALLY WITH CHRISTIAN PROFESSIONAL ORGANIZATIONS

There are also national and international Christian professional organizations that can provide encouragement and connect you with Christians in your profession locally. (This list is not intended as an endorsement of these individual ministries.)

Christian Veterinarian Mission (christianvetmission.org) networks professionals in veterinary medicine.

Christian Legal Society (clsnet.org) networks attorneys, judges, law professors, law students, and others in the legal system.

Affiliation of Christian Engineers (christianengineer.net) provides numerous ways to network and obtain information relevant to the profession of engineering and to the common faith of those who work in this profession.

Christian Leadership Ministries (clm.org) is Campus Crusade's ministry to university professors.

Christian Medical & Dental Associations (cmds.org) is a ministry to and network of medical professionals in the United States.

International Health Services (ihserve.org) is a ministry to health care professionals internationally.

International Medical and Dental Association (cmf.org.uk/icmda) is an association of national Christian medical and dental societies in over sixty countries.

InterVarsity Grad and Faculty Ministry (ivcf.org/grad) networks university faculty and graduate students.

Nurses Christian Fellowship (ivcf.org/ncf) is InterVarsity's ministry to the nursing profession.

Fellowship of Christian Physician Assistants (fcpa.net) works to support Christian PAs in their efforts to incorporate their faith into their practices.

Christian Businessmen's Committee (www.cbmc.com) networks Christians in business.

The Christian Working Woman (christianworkingwoman.org) is a ministry dedicated to equipping and encouraging Christian women in the workplace.

Fellowship of Companies for Christ International (myfcci.org) networks CEOs, presidents, and leaders of family businesses.

Business & Professional Ministries—a ministry of the Navigators (bpnavigators.org) helps business and professional workers extend their faith to their family, their peers, and their community.

Christians in Commerce (christiansincommerce.org) is a nationwide network of primarily Roman Catholic business leaders.

Priority Associates (priorityassociates.org) is Campus Crusade's international ministry to and with marketplace Christians.

Marketplace Ministries (www.marketplaceministries.com) provides chaplains for on-site Employee Assistance programs for companies. (Your company may want to consider hiring a company chaplain to minister to the needs of your people.)

Christian Business Alliance supports Christians in business in Great Britain. Contact the alliance at The Pickenham Centre, North Pickenham, Swaffham, Norfolk, England, PE3 8LG. Phone (01760) 440561; fax (01760) 440561.

Council of Christians in Commerce is a London-based network of believers. Contact the council at 51 Peverells Wood Ave., Chandlers Ford, Eastleigh, Hampshire England, SO5 2BS.

PICKING YOUR TEAM

- Identify the part you can best play, given your skills, abilities, and resources.
- Identify the kind of team support you need.
- Evaluate the gifts and resources of your immediate contacts.
- Identify those who have the skills and experience to meet the needs of the people you influence.

Potential Team Members

_____   _____

_____   _____

_____   _____

_____   _____

THE BOTTOM LINE

Evangelism is a team activity. No one can do it all. Learn to work with others for maximum spiritual impact.

Evangelism by
Walking Around

Distance is dead.[1] Colin Powell knows it. The acclaimed army commander and secretary of state under United States President George W. Bush is one of the most respected leaders in the world. No matter what his rank during his distinguished military career, Powell thrived and depended on honest dialogue. He said, "The day soldiers stop bringing you their problems is the day you stop leading them."[2] As a military leader he wanted all his soldiers to know that he genuinely wanted to hear what was on their minds.

According to Powell, the quickest way to kill communication—whether leading soldiers or running the State Department—is to park himself behind a massive desk. As a soldier, he maintained accessibility, habitually taking an afternoon walk and allowing himself to be "ambushed." He wanted to see firsthand what was going on throughout his command. What's more, a soldier of any rank had access to him during what he called his "outside office hours" without having to run the gauntlet of his staff.

Powell certainly wanted his soldiers to know he cared, but his walks were about much more than morale. When Powell took over the reins of the State Department, he shared this thought with his staff:

> You will find an open style, you will find me bouncing in, you will find me wanting to talk to desk officers. I want to hear the rough edges of all arguments. I don't want to concur things to death and coordinate things to death so I get a round pebble instead of a stone that has edges on it. I want to get all the great ideas that exist throughout the Department.[3]

Powell understands that business is not just business; it's personal. His perspective on leadership has a distinct personal twist to it: "Leadership is motivating people, turning people on, getting 110 percent out of a personal relationship."[4] Hooray for Powell!

Distance is dead. Business guru Tom Peters made the point in his book *The Circle of Innovation*, and he reinforced it in his book *A Passion for Excellence.* Peters and coauthor Nancy Austin conclude that the number one productivity problem in America is managers who are out of touch with their people and their customers.[5] Their remedy is what they call MBWA — *management by walking around.* How does it work? You get out of *your* office enough to know what's going on as you observe and listen to customers, to employees, and to anyone who's an important part of one's business. The book raises tough issues about executive isolation in the workplace and even suggests that supervisors who don't know their employees' first and last names should be fired.[6]

Thankfully, God doesn't fire us when we fail to connect with our coworkers, but make no mistake: Distance is dead in evangelism. Knowing people's names, concerns, and problems is as important for any person who wants to have a spiritual impact on a coworker as it is for a supervisor who wants the most productive operation possible.

Distance is dead. God knows it. He's always known it. Rather than camping behind a celestial desk, Jesus came to earth for a little MBWA of his own:

> [Christ Jesus], being in very nature God,
>   did not consider equality with God something to be grasped,
> but made himself nothing,
>   taking the very nature of a servant,
> being made in human likeness.
>
> Philippians 2:6–7

For more than thirty years Jesus lived and felt our world. Far from keeping himself in isolation, he experienced it all:

> [Jesus] had to be made like his brothers in every way, in order that he might become a merciful and faithful high priest in service to God,

and that he might make atonement for the sins of the people. Because he himself suffered when he was tempted, he is able to help those who are being tempted.

Hebrews 2:17–18

Distance is dead. Well, it's dead everywhere—except maybe in the church. Almost everyone else seems to understand it, yet many Christians still aren't getting it. It seems to us that some religious leaders work overtime to get people through the doors of the church—as many days a week as possible—for worship, prayer meetings, fellowship dinners, and other activities. We're not saying Christian fellowship at church is wrong. Far from it. After all, the Bible teaches, "Let us not give up meeting together, as some are in the habit of doing" (Hebrews 10:25). But Jesus taught his followers that their place was "in the world." To his heavenly Father he prayed:

My prayer is not that you take them out of the world but that you protect them from the evil one. They are not of the world, even as I am not of it. Sanctify them by the truth; your word is truth. As you sent me into the world, I have sent them into the world.

John 17:15–18

Sometimes we think the church has forgotten that Jesus was a friend of sinners (see Matthew 9:10–11), not a friend of the synagogue. Of course, there are exceptions, but evangelism from a distance is a concept foreign to the Bible and to the early Christians. We've got to understand: *There is no impact without contact.*

Sadly, within two to three years of their conversion, new Christians typically lose significant contact with nonbelieving friends; a host of new Christian friends and activities can consume their schedules. Take Barbara for example. Though Jill and Barbara had never worked together, they really hit it off when they were paired up on the Richardson account. The urgency of their report threw them together for an intense three weeks. During that time, different spiritual issues came up in the course of natural conversation, and Jill seemed genuinely interested in Barbara's perspective. They decided to treat themselves to lunch when they completed their work.

Over lunch they discovered that they both loved tennis but hardly ever played anymore. They pulled out their calendars. When Jill suggested Sunday morning, she discovered that Barbara went to church then—and also on Sunday evening. Saturday morning? Barbara had a leaders' meeting for a Bible study, which also eliminated Wednesday evening, the night of the study. Jill attended class on Tuesday and Thursday nights. Monday? Barbara attended a prayer group. Neither of them wanted to make a standing commitment on Friday or Saturday night, so Barbara, not wanting the opportunity to slip away, asked Jill to go to church with her. Jill politely declined, and Barbara left assuming that Jill just wasn't interested in spiritual things.

No Impact without Contact

Expressing our faith with grace in the workplace is not about techniques, systems, or method; it's not about overwork, but an overflow from a life in which God is actively at work. But to open yourself up to the kind of personal observation of your life that people need, you must intentionally spend meaningful time with non-Christians. You can be the most winsome, godly person in your workplace, but if people aren't able to observe you in close proximity and then investigate your life by asking questions, they won't benefit from your presence.

If you allow your schedule to be filled with organized religious or church activities, leaving no time to bridge the distance between yourself and non-Christians, you're failing to fulfill your calling. If your busy spiritual schedule crowds out the possibility of spending time with people outside the faith, you may want to ask yourself how Christlike you are.

There's a delicate balance between spending time with fellow followers of Jesus and spending time with non-Christians. If I put a distance between non-Christians and myself, I'm sacrificing an important part of my ability to influence them spiritually. In fact, spending too much time in the "holy huddle" can produce a legalistic, critical attitude toward others that few find attractive. I have an essential message, but no one is listening. I can become a spiritual porcupine that repels unbelievers.

There's a corresponding danger, though, of overidentifying with non-Christians to the point that I become so assimilated that my life has no message. In this case I have an audience, but no message. I have become a spiritual chameleon that changes color to match whatever group he's with. If we are committed to growing spiritually—becoming attractive, Christlike persons—we *do* need to spend time with other believers. Each of us brings to the mix something that another Christian needs in order to grow: "Speaking the truth in love, we will in all things grow up into him who is the Head, that is, Christ. From him the whole body, joined and held together by every supporting ligament, grows and builds itself up in love, as each part does its work" (Ephesians 4:15–16).

> Oftentimes, I see Christians who really are not willing to invest maybe five or ten years in a relationship with a non-Christian; rather they will spend most of their time with Christians. So they never build the authentic relationships, and to the extent that they are not pursuing excellence in their work, they really don't have a platform for impact.
>
> *Jack Alexander, travel and hospitality industry*

Distance is dead! At least as far as the New Testament is concerned. Christians are consistently encouraged to bridge the distance, to build common ground with non-Christians. We like how the Living Bible paraphrases Paul's thoughts:

> When with the heathen I agree with them as much as I can, except of course that I must always do what is right as a Christian. And so, by agreeing, I can win their confidence and help them too.
>
> When I am with those whose consciences bother them easily, I don't act as though I know it all and don't say they are foolish; the result is that they are willing to let me help them. Yes, whatever a person is like, I try to find common ground with him so that he will let me tell him about Christ and let Christ save him.
>
> 1 Corinthians 9:21–22 LB

It's sometimes said that Christian and non-Christians have little in common. While it's true we have a different belief system and lifestyle, there are a lot of commonalties that can help us bridge the differences. Making time in your schedule for non-Christian coworkers demands careful thinking, a conviction that it's time well spent, and at times a willingness to take risks.

INVEST IN COMMON GROUND

Common ground is simply a shared area of life. You already share one huge area of common ground with prebelievers—your workplace. In a sense, this entire book deals with ways to capitalize on this reality. As you intentionally engage in the cultivation phase of evangelism with as many people as possible, you may discover that there are a few individuals who respond more favorably to you personally. Consider investing more time with these people in order to discover other areas of common ground:

COMMON INTERESTS

Sports, fishing, boating, reading, politics—what interests do you share with others? I (Bill) have a friend who is constantly on the lookout for a few men who love golf. About four times a year, he gathers up a foursome. On his private plane they take a long-distance golf trip, during which they always get around to discussing golf—and Jesus.

I (Bill) love fly-fishing. There's nothing like being out in a remote area on a cold mountain stream to stir my blood. When I have a friend along to share this experience, it's even better. Nothing is as natural as talking about the Creator when surrounded by his beautiful creation. No telling where a conversation will lead after a long day on the river.

For years, I (Walt) developed hobbies by intentionally learning from pre-Christians. From bird-watching to Rotary Club to growing orchids, I was able to purposefully choose to learn and practice these interests with Christians *and* non-Christians. These activities resulted in relationships that grew deeper as I saw people making many mini-decisions that for some resulted in their coming to trust Jesus.

As you become acquainted with others at work, watch for common interests. You don't have to pack more into an already busy schedule if you can include non-Christians in your established activities. And don't think it has to be something exotic. Do you know a few people who share a love for the sports team that made it to the Super Bowl or World Series? Throw a party and watch the game together. Even if you never talk about anything spiritual, they'll get to know and, we hope, trust you a little more. And you'll put to rest the rumor that Christians don't have fun.

Next time you go to a movie, instead of just going by yourself, think about others who might enjoy seeing what you're planning to see. Occasionally a movie picks up biblical themes that make it easy to turn the conversation to spiritual matters without seeming pushy. Or invite a coworker and family over for dinner. Don't push anything or feel frustrated if you don't talk about spiritual topics. Just sharing a meal with someone fosters a sense of relationship and can lead to spiritual conversation later.

COMMON NEEDS

Common needs can sometimes draw you together. If you drive a substantial distance to work, consider posting a carpool notice on an employee information board. At the same time you're saving money and reducing air pollution, you may discover a new venue in which to discuss spiritually significant issues. Be sure not to force conversation on a captive audience, or you may quickly find your car pool reduced to one person.

Hear about a coworker who's moving? Help organize a group of fellow workers to lend a hand. It says "I care" and can produce camaraderie and teamwork that can flow back into workplace cooperation. Listen for opportunities to offer a special expertise or just a strong back.

I (Walt) have discovered an interesting connection between a need and someone else's ability to help. For years I thought the way into a person's life was always to be on the giving end. But when I allow someone to make an investment in my life, he or she becomes vested in me. My wife, Barb, and I were devastated to find out our first child had cerebral palsy (damage to the brain had occurred before she was born). The resulting delays in Kate's physical and mental development required Barb and me to seek out a number of folks—virtually all were non-Christians—to help us out. These prolonged relationships allowed us to cultivate and to plant spiritual seeds.

While it is undeniably true that many people find it incredibly difficult to allow others to help them with a need, this common ground can be a fertile one for cultivation.

COMMON GIFTS AND TALENTS

Common abilities often draw people together. Whether it's a work-related ability, love of music, or playing a sport well, common gifts provide an opportunity to work, play, and create together that can foster relationships. One physician organized a jazz band of other talented doctors, several of whom were non-Christians, who loved music. Playing together has created opportunities to talk about spiritual things.

How about organizing a company sports team? Although some churches require their sports team members to attend a particular number of services per month, we know of a few that want at least 50 percent of their roster to be made up of non-Christians. Christians who want to be part of the team have to invite a person who doesn't attend church. If it's true, as some have said, that you can learn more about a person in five minutes of play than in an hour of work, then pursuing recreational opportunities with non-Christians is one of the most neglected strategies for showing people the love of Jesus.

COMMON LOCATION

Working in proximity to someone else throws you into the other's world naturally. It's no accident that you work next to these particular men and women. The same is true for the neighborhood in which you live—or perhaps the restaurants you frequent or any of the service providers you use.

COMMON CONCERNS

Similar life situations often create opportunities to develop meaningful relationships. Nothing has the connecting ability quite like the common concern parents have for their children. Children draw people together. Parents like nothing better than to talk about their kids. And there is nothing like a parental struggle and search for answers to make a person's heart tender.

Similar family situations create all kinds of opportunities. Barb led a Girl Scout group with several of Walt's business associates who had daughters. I (Bill) coached a Little League team for years that opened many doors for meaningful relationships and conversations.

As you discover and invest time in this area—and all these areas of common ground—your immediate spiritual goal is not to harvest but to cultivate. The more time someone spends with you, the more time he or she has to observe the difference Jesus is making in your life. As a relationship develops, meaningful communication will take place, softening hard soil and providing a means through which biblical truth can later be exchanged. Without common ground, we are left trying to cope with the distance factor.

CONTACT WITH CONTAMINATION

If our faith is authentic and attractive, people will want to spend time with us. If they feel safe around us, they'll want to invite us into their world—a world filled with actions, activities, and conversations that can sometimes be offensive to those of us who follow Jesus.

At times it can be dangerous. Even the most devoted Christian can be tempted to do something he or she knows is wrong. It's the reason new Christians are often encouraged to put some distance between themselves and their old non-Christian friends. And there are, of course, times when a bridge to the old way of life must be burned. In his letter to Timothy, Paul warns, "Flee the evil desires of youth, and pursue righteousness, faith, love and peace, along with those who call on the Lord out of a pure heart" (2 Timothy 2:22). Paul writes this about greed and the love of money: "But you, man of God, flee from all this, and pursue righteousness, godliness, faith, love, endurance and gentleness" (1 Timothy 6:11).

Not long ago a new acquaintance of mine (Bill) was helping a female friend move from one apartment to another. He had a truck; she had a need. Great opportunity! Maybe there would be a chance to talk about Jesus. Things went well until she offered to return the favor—sexually. Having come out of a sexually active background, this new follower of Jesus had enough sense to know he would be no match for the magnetism of the flesh if he were to stay. So he left abruptly and angered his friend in the process. In this case, any concern about setting the relationship back becomes secondary. He may have burned the bridge, but had he succumbed to temptation and maintained the bridge, he would have had very little in the way of Christlikeness—integrity, holiness, purity—to carry across. Losing our integrity to maintain the bridge is too dear a price to pay.

It's also best to break relationships built around illegal activity, no matter how much you care about former partners in crime. These relationships can be difficult to break, even when someone wants to. Recently a man we know became a follower of Jesus. He was part of an organized crime syndicate. Continuing a relationship with his former associates would require him to be a part of illegal activities; breaking off the relationship could mean death. He concluded that the God who loved him enough to die for him could take care of him, and he told his colleagues he couldn't maintain contact with them. We're still praying for his safety and the salvation of his former friends.

Far too often, however, old bridges are burned or new walls erected needlessly by Christians over the sin they encounter in non-Christians. The Bible is clear that, except in extreme cases, burning bridges is not an option for followers of Jesus. The apostle Paul counsels the Corinthian believers to separate from immoral persons *in the church*. He does not advise that they automatically dissociate themselves from non-Christians: "I have written you in my letter not to associate with sexually immoral people—not at all meaning the people of this world who are immoral, or the greedy and swindlers, or idolaters. In that case you would have to leave this world" (1 Corinthians 5:9–10). The way Jesus spent his time reveals that he not only associated with sinners, he made it a priority.

BUILDING BRIDGES, NOT WALLS

It's important to be honest here. Walls are much easier to build than bridges. It's true in construction, and it's true in relationships. Yet, when it comes to relationships with non-Christians, we want to build bridges, not walls.

Both of us have pre-Christian friends who practice sinful lifestyles. We haven't hidden where we stand, but we've worked at communicating what we believe in ways that do not build walls. What do we do when we encounter destructive, sinful behavior in the non-Christians we befriend? And how do we connect with them without being contaminated ourselves or appearing to approve behavior that is definitely sinful when measured against God's Word?

FACING OFFENSIVE BEHAVIOR INOFFENSIVELY

There are a number of helpful principles to follow in learning how to face offensive behavior inoffensively:

Don't Be Surprised at People's Sinfulness

The longer we both live, the more evidence we collect that men and women are lost and broken creatures trying to eke out an existence in a world that doesn't make sense to them. Ponder this. If a thirsty individual believes there is no other option, he or she will try to find a drink, even if it's from a polluted stream. Why, then, would we expect a person who does not know God to abandon the hope of worldly fulfillment with no prospect of filling that gnawing thirst in his or her soul?

I (Bill) once attended a workshop where pretty normal-looking people were offered the opportunity to come clean about their shortcomings and failures in a spiritually safe environment. When some of them shared their sins, I had to catch myself from staring in disbelief — "I can't believe you did that." I don't think I'll ever look at an audience again without being reminded that a world of pain, sin, and failure is looking back at me, searching for hope.

We are prone to be surprised at people's sinfulness when we forget two things: (1) how lost the human race really is, and (2) how personally sinful we have been and can still choose to be — underestimating our potential for wickedness and overestimating our innate goodness.

Expressing observable dismay at another person's sin is tantamount to saying, "I don't believe what the Bible says." It also communicates to unbelievers, "I'm better than you." This is, of course, not true, and it builds a wall that's hard to tear down. A lot of the self-righteous hypocrisy with which Christians are labeled starts right here—when we become surprised at people's sinfulness.

Put the Holy Spirit in Charge of Cleanup

Remember, conviction is *not* your job. Jesus gave that job to the Holy Spirit (see John 16:8). Guilt and shame induced by human beings is far less persuasive and is usually viewed as arrogance or judgment.

Having grown up in East Texas, where there's a church on every corner, I (Bill) had no shortage of human pressure to get right with God. We had an expression for this kind of goodness: "He was starched before he was washed." When we try to starch people—get them to conform to our set of behaviors—before they've been washed— become a new person in Christ—everyone is uncomfortable.

I am continually amazed at Jesus' and the early church leaders' ability to overlook outward sinful behavior. They didn't do so because they were soft on sin. They were interested in something deeper than behavior change, namely, *heart-level transformation.* They knew that until the heart changed, they could rail against sin all day long and make no real progress. When the apostle Paul entered a city, in a culture more decadent than ours, he didn't preach to nonbelievers about moral issues. He offered a relationship with God through Jesus—a relationship that can change people to the very core of their being. He focused on Jesus and let the Holy Spirit do the cleanup.

Leave Your Reputation in God's Hands

Don't be afraid of being called a friend of sinners. Sometimes the way the King James Version puts 1 Thessalonians 5:22 ("Abstain from all appearance of evil") is taken as a warning about getting too close to sinners. Some spiritual leaders teach that hanging out with the wrong kind of people in the wrong places will give the appearance of acceptance of certain activities. Here's a common example they use: sitting at a bar, even though you don't drink, could give the appearance that you condone drinking—or even that you yourself have been drinking. The New International Version translates this verse, "Avoid *every kind of evil*" (italics added)—not *everything that might be mistaken for* evil. If we live in a constant state of worry over what everybody else thinks, we deny both Jesus' and Paul's examples of relating to nonbelievers.

If you spend time with sinners, be prepared. Modern-day Pharisees will attack you. Take heart, though. Neither Jesus nor Paul cared about what the legalists thought. Both, however, were concerned about their reputation among one group—non-Christians. Paul urges the Colossian believers, "Be wise in the way you act toward outsiders; make the most of every opportunity" (Colossians 4:5). And in his letter to the Thessalonians he tells believers, "Make it your ambition to lead a quiet life, to mind your own business and to work with your hands, just as we told you, so that your daily life may win the respect of outsiders and so that you will not be dependent on anybody" (1 Thessalonians 4:11–12). Paul even points to reputation with nonbelievers as a requirement for church leadership: "[The overseer] must also have a good reputation with outsiders, so that he will not fall into disgrace and into the devil's trap" (1 Timothy 3:7).

It hurts when someone attacks us, especially when our motives are misjudged. But it's awfully hard to please legalists anyway. Their self-esteem is built on their own sense of superiority. Trying to please porcupine Christians usually leads to behavior that damages your relationship with nonbelievers—the very people Jesus prayed you would spend time with.

Make Your Choices Based on Biblical Truth, Not Opinion

Paul makes it clear that sincere believers can differ on the amount of freedom they have in living as a Christian. Yet in his letter to the Romans he says that we have no right to impose our convictions on someone else, but rather that all of us must evaluate our standards by God's Word:

> The man who eats everything must not look down on him who does not, and the man who does not eat everything must not condemn the man who does, for God has accepted him. Who are you to

judge someone else's servant? To his own master he stands or falls. And he will stand, for the Lord is able to make him stand.

One man considers one day more sacred than another; another man considers every day alike. Each one should be fully convinced in his own mind.

Romans 14:3–5

Here's a way of looking at things that has helped us. There are three kinds of activities: (1) things that are always wrong, (2) things that are right, and (3) things that are disputable. There is such a thing as right and wrong. Some things are always wrong, not because God arbitrarily decided to make a list of sins, but because the behavior is contrary to who God is. No good motive can wipe out the fact that certain actions are always sinful—no matter what our rationale is or how much we rationalize it. C. S. Lewis had it right: "No clever arrangement of bad eggs ever made a good omelet."

Things we do that are good and right are good and right because they correspond to who God is and what he has commanded. Nevertheless, unlike the bad things (which are always wrong, no matter what our motive is), our attitude or motive *can* contaminate good actions. We can do good things for wrong or bad motives—and that makes them wrong for us. There are also lots of behaviors that the Bible never speaks about directly or indirectly. It's about these disputable issues that Paul says, "Each one should be fully convinced in his own mind" (Romans 14:5). We need to be very careful about adding rules for Christian living that the Bible never mentions.

SAYING NO WITH GRACE

A few years ago a Christian businessman accepted an invitation to attend the Masters golf tournament. He flew with a group of men on the host's private jet to Augusta, where they enjoyed an incredible day, watching the PGA's finest golfers. The problem came at day's end, when the host suggested that they make a stop at a topless bar before the flight home.

Assuming you'd be uncomfortable with that, what would you have done in that situation? To up the ante, let's say you had had several conversations about spiritual topics with one of the other guests. He had shown an interest, and you sensed he was moving toward a relationship with Jesus. Should you go along and say nothing for fear of reversing the progress you'd made thus far not only with your host but with the other guest? Or should you announce that the activity is sinful and therefore refuse to go?

We suggest neither approach. When someone invites you to participate in an activity you know you should avoid, you can turn down the offer gracefully. You don't have to be belligerent or defensive. Communicate your choice simply and without explanation—or with as little explanation as possible.

Here are some guidelines to help you express grace rather than judgment when you receive an invitation to participate in something you consider sinful.

Recognize the Intent of the Invitation

When non-Christian friends invite us to do things we consider off-limits, it's usually not intended as a setup to tempt us to sin. In most cases our friends want to share something they enjoy. The intention is good, even if the suggested action isn't. This good intention is something we can appreciate even if we can't participate. If the invitation is a test of some sort, however, that's another matter. In this case it's time to take a stand and say that as a Christian you don't feel comfortable engaging in that activity.

Offer an Acceptable Alternative

If the offer is one of genuine friendship, it may be that it isn't the particular suggested activity that is the issue. The person may just want to spend time with you. Some non-Christian friends of mine (Walt) asked Barb and me to a movie one night—a movie we felt it would be wrong for us to attend. Rather than making a big deal about it, I said simply, "We'd love to go to the movies with you guys, but Barb has really wanted to see _____ [I named another movie]. Have you seen that one yet? We've heard that it's great." It turned out that they didn't care what movie we saw. They just wanted to spend an evening with us—their new friends. And yes, later that night over a cup of coffee, we discussed the movie and some pretty significant spiritual issues.

Watch the Excuses

With the one exception—when someone is intentionally trying to get us to violate our conscience—there is wisdom in declining to use our faith as an excuse for abstaining from an activity. If we're not careful, we may end up adding one more piece of evidence to someone's conviction that following Jesus is only about keeping a set of strict rules. Christians in America today are defined more by what they don't do than by what they do. To counter this gross misperception, we suggest not pouring more fuel on the fire by pointing to God as the reason we are not participating, unless forced to do so by a direct challenge to our faith.

Remember That God Is Gracious

God went out of his way to draw us to himself, despite the sinfulness that clings to us. When our response to a well-intended invitation sounds narrow and judgmental, it's reasonable to ask why someone would want a relationship with us in the first place. God's judgment didn't draw us. His love and grace did. We need to follow God's example and return the favor by being gracious to others.

Distance is dead. Let's keep it that way. And so let's be careful not to add needlessly to the divide between Christians and non-Christians. As we close the gap, building relational bridges, we can be part of the great cultivating work of preparing hearts to receive Jesus.

THE BOTTOM LINE												
If we want to influence people, we can close the distance by spending time with them developing and enjoying common ground.												

How to Walk through
an Open Door

In our teaching we have found that people often become anxious because we spend so much time discussing the cultivation stage. This reaction is quite understandable. After all, the whole point of cultivating a field is to grow and harvest a crop. People want to know, "When do we get to plant?"

The evangelism process, like the agricultural process, invests the majority of its time and energy in preparing the soil—joining the Lord in the cultivation of the heart to receive the seed of God's word. The simple truth is that the more time and energy you invest in cultivation, the more opportunity you will have to plant and reap—and the better the soil, the more fruitful the harvest.

Our immediate goal with people is not to lead them to Jesus but consistently to take the initiative to join them in the places where God is working in their lives and to help them take the next step in their journeys toward faith. As you look at the "Microdecisions of Faith" chart on page 24, note that there is more to this process than moving from one step to the next. Cultivation is never an end in itself. As trust is developed and God softens the human heart, we look for opportunities to plant the seeds of biblical truth.

As people feel themselves moving closer to a personal relationship with God, their resistance often increases. Not only may the enemy of their souls be sensing defeat, but they might have legitimate intellectual questions. In fact, we know we've entered the planting stage—the communication of biblical truth—when we encounter the challenge of the intellectual barrier. (This is the point at which many evangelism courses begin.)

In this chapter, we move from the cultivation to the planting phase. We emphasize that the boundary between the two stages is by no means hard and fast. That is, even after we begin to impart spiritual truth, continuing to build trust remains crucial. Keep in mind that planting involves far more than a onetime walk through the facts of the gospel. It entails helping a person address sincere, well-founded, and perhaps long-standing intellectual questions about faith issues. This takes time. So as we plant truth, we continue to cultivate. Just as in agriculture, the two phases overlap.

SOIL ANALYSIS

Soil analysis in the planting phase revolves largely around the intellectual barrier, which might be defined as a predisposition to disregard or reject Christianity as false, irrelevant, or merely a human social construct. The most fundamental reason for this pre-disposition is *ignorance*—a lack of knowledge about the Bible and the truth it offers. See the chart on page 24.

Remember my (Bill's) story about my airplane conversation (page 47–48)? Even though this highly intelligent young woman had been raised in the Bible Belt, I found almost no common intellectual ground from which to start a discussion. We're encountering more and more people who are, for all intents and purposes, biblically illiterate. They need both good information and nonthreatening ways to investigate what the Bible says about who they are, who Jesus is, and what he has done for them.

Biblical ignorance is compounded by erroneous beliefs. Many hold *misconceptions* about Christianity, often viewing religion largely in terms of what adherents are supposed to *do* for God or for the church. They have never considered the Bible's relevance for their lives.

This focus on performing in the name of religion stems in part from human beings' innate desire to prove ourselves worthy. Religious organizations and churches can sometimes feed this proclivity by focusing on how they can get individuals to serve their organizational needs. The result is that when we try to discuss spiritual things, people sometimes assume we're talking about additional obligations and oppressive responsibilities to an authoritarian institution. Not surprisingly, they view these perceived obligations and responsibilities as irrelevant, if not potentially dangerous.

The true essence of the Christian faith is, of course, radically different from the perception just described. Jesus comes to a person and says, "Let me tell you what's in it for you. I'm going to be gracious to you. I don't want anything from you but your love and trust. Let me show you how to really live life to the full." This is a key distinction between Christianity and other faiths. Christianity is primarily about what *God has done* for us, not what *we do* for him. It's not about how we qualify for membership or acceptance; it's not about becoming better. It's about trusting and obeying God in an intensely personal relationship made possible by the sacrifice of Jesus. A relationship with God is not a purchase; it's not earned. It's a response to a free gift.

The soil of a person's mind can become tainted in different ways. Some rejected the Bible in college as they were confronted with a naturalistic intellectualism that challenged any and all supernatural worldviews. At Southern Methodist University in the late 1960s, I (Bill) took a class called "The Nature of Man," which seemed to me to be designed to erode the faith of mushy-minded freshmen by undermining any confidence a person might have had in the Bible. Fortunately, several campus ministries helped me lay truth side by side with error. When that happens, guess which one always wins? Error is no match for truth. But had I had no access to truth, the error would have seemed very convincing. Israel's King Solomon understood this: "The first to present his case seems right, till another comes forward and questions him" (Proverbs 18:17). No wonder people who have never been exposed to a reasonable defense of the supernatural stumble intellectually when they come face-to-face with the gospel.

One of the greatest shortcomings of evangelicalism in America has been a distrust of human intellect. True, modernism put too much trust in human intelligence. But an unequivocal distrust of human reason and intellectual pursuits constitutes an overreaction. Paul calls for the mind to be *renewed*, not discarded. Without the exercise of the mind, implies Paul, it would be impossible to test and approve God's will: "Do not conform any longer to the pattern of this world, but be transformed by the renewing of your mind. Then you will be able to test and approve what God's will is—his good, pleasing and perfect will" (Romans 12:2).

SOIL TREATMENT

People whose minds are tainted with spiritual ignorance and error often progress toward spiritual *indifference*, which can eventually spawn hostility toward faith, especially if the condition is left untreated. However, a thoughtful presentation of biblical truth in the context of a meaningful relationship—a presentation that challenges the mind to consider Jesus and his claims—is the perfect "soil treatment." This is the work we call planting, and it occurs when the seed of biblical truth is spread in love and with compassion to hearts that, because they have been cultivated, are receptive.

TIME FOR THOUGHT

- Make a list of your coworkers who may be struggling at the intellectual level.
- What obstacles do you see in their way?

THE OPEN DOOR

The overriding goal of the planting phase is for a colleague to gain *understanding*. It is not—repeat, *not*—to win an argument. In cultivation, we pray to understand non-Christian colleagues as part of building a relationship of trust. In planting, we pray they come to recognize and begin to understand what the Bible has to say about life.

In this and later chapters, we'll discuss in greater detail options and resources for effective planting. For now, however, we simply note that in one-on-one discussions with prebelievers, a key to effective communication of spiritual truth is keeping the metaphor of the *open door* at the forefront of our thinking. Paul uses this metaphor as he writes to believers in Colossae: "And pray for us, too, that God may open a door for our message, so that we may proclaim the mystery of Christ, for which I am in chains" (Colossians 4:3).

Imagine you are walking down the hall at your workplace. You pass office after office inhabited by coworkers. You choose a door on which to knock. You hear your coworker come to the door. He cracks the door open and peers out. What you say next will make all the difference in the world. If you say, "If you were to die tonight, would you spend your eternity with Jesus in heaven, or would you burn in hell?" the door will most likely slam. On the other hand, if he expects a stimulating, nonjudgmental discussion about something he judges to be important, the door may open a bit more.

In our "planting" conversations, we can envision our friends opening or shutting their minds, just as they would open or shut a door. As they open the door, they invite us to take more time, as the opportunity may arise, to discuss biblical truth. If they shut the door in response to us, we've aided them in raising intellectual or emotional barriers against Jesus.

> I have prayed that God would help me see whether somebody is ready to go further or has a curiosity, and that I would have the courage at that moment to proceed. When people ask me questions that seem to head in that direction, I am willing to go one step further and see what the response is.
>
> *Marvin N. Schoenhals,*
> *financial services*

As the order of Paul's request to the Colossians implies, you can be bold and clear, and even wise and winsome, but if the door is shut, the mind is closed — and you can expect a negative response.

RECOGNIZING OPEN DOORS

An open door is simply an opportunity to talk more seriously about Jesus or the Bible at the invitation of the listener. Usually these opportunities occur after a prolonged time of cultivation. How do you recognize when coworkers are opening a spiritual door and inviting more discussion? Here are some helpful suggestions:

Ask Questions

Ask — and then actively listen. Don't yield to the temptation to talk about yourself. When we're looking for a conversational door to walk through, monopolizing the conversation with our choice of subjects can work against us, whereas if we focus on the other person, the conversational door invariably opens further. My (Bill's) wife, Kathy, says there are two kinds of people—the "here I am" person and the "there you are" person. We want to be "there you are" people by asking questions about a person's favorite subject, which is, of course, himself or herself.

One of my (Walt's) favorite colleagues, Joseph Lieberman, MD, coauthored a book titled *The Fifteen Minute Hour*[1] in which he teaches physicians to use an acrostic (BATHE) to learn a lot about a patient in a short time—in other words, to open doors sensitively and effectively.

- Background. Start BATHEing by asking a question such as "What's been going on in your life?" If the person begins to open the door, you could ask, "Could you give me some more background?" or say, "Tell me more about this."
- Affect. Instead of quickly giving advice, an answer, or a Bible verse, ask, "How is this affecting you?" or "How is this affecting your family?" or "How do you feel about what's going on?" or "How is this affecting your mood?" This gives your friend an opportunity to go beyond just the facts and to report how she is really feeling.
- Trouble. Then ask, "What is troubling you the most about this?" You're beginning now to get to the problem and to allow the door to open wider.
- Handling. "How are you handling things?" gives you a feel for how your friend is coping with the situation; it may give you a key as to the direction you can suggest for help.
- Empathy. Here you demonstrate empathic compassion. Saying "It must be an incredibly difficult thing to face" or "I can't imagine how tough this is for you" legitimizes the person's feelings and provides the support they need and want.

The BATHE acrostic in essence encourages you to *ask* and *listen*. It doesn't expect you to be a rescuer or a "Dear Abby" advice giver. At the same time, it allows the other person to open a door to you and provide you with insight into the needs he or she is experiencing—needs into which you will, when asked, be able to plant biblical truth.

Listen for Expressions of Felt Needs

As you begin to get to know someone better, he or she may, for example, mention a struggle with children, a boss, or an employee. When someone expresses a need, it almost always indicates that this person is looking for meaningful answers to life's problems. By intentionally entering each workday appointment, encounter, or conversation asking WIGD?—What is God doing?—and keeping your spiritual antennae tuned for divine appointments, you may find that these conversations can take on a whole new meaning.

WALKING THROUGH OPEN DOORS

Following are six principles to consider when you begin to hear the squeak of an opening door. By observing these simple guidelines, you can walk through an open door with the truth and, one hopes, keep the door open for more in-depth discussion:

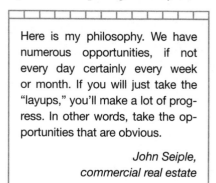

Here is my philosophy. We have numerous opportunities, if not every day certainly every week or month. If you will just take the "layups," you'll make a lot of progress. In other words, take the opportunities that are obvious.

John Seiple,
commercial real estate

Principle 1: Proceed Slowly

This is a difficult principle for both of us to practice. Because of our ministry and counseling experience (and because we are men who instinctively want to "fix" things), we're naturally tempted to rush in and give advice or share scriptural principles. We've both needed to listen to the Spirit's whisper: "Careful. Slow down. Don't get ahead of me!"

Principle 2: Ask Permission to Speak Further

We can talk to others about almost any subject (including religion and politics) as long as we're willing to speak with respect and sensitivity—and as long as we ask permission: "Can I share something I've learned about that?" or, "Can I tell you a story about some help I got with a similar problem?" With permission, we can confidently share faith stories, knowing that it's not likely that the door will slam in our faces.

Principle 3: Be Sensitive to Your Listeners

Watch for verbal and nonverbal cues that the door remains open or that it is beginning to close. Be careful about using religious jargon. And also remember the clock. You can always schedule more time to meet later—which is especially important when you're talking with someone in the workplace. Don't abuse company time. Schedule a lunch or talk further at a break or after work if necessary.

Principle 4: Check Regularly to See If Your Listeners Are Still with You

This principle takes us back to "ask, ask, ask." Most of what we do in the planting stage involves *dialogue*—not preaching or teaching. We ask and listen, we share and understand. You simply can't do that if the conversation is one-way. When you check to see if your friend is hearing you clearly, and when you make sure that you're hearing her clearly, you are practicing genuine communication.

Principle 5: Regulate the Dosage

Take one step at a time. Intriguing people with a little truth that leaves them wanting more is better than overpowering them with more than they can process. One of the most freeing things we as witnesses can do is leave the results to God. By not taking responsibility for God's work, we are free to allow the Holy Spirit to set the schedule. Doing so allows us to apply small amounts of seed and water and then leave the rest to the Lord.

Principle 6: Don't React Negatively to Objections

Recognize the role that doubt can play in a person's life. Don't forget that the emotional obstacles we sometimes see in the cultivation phase of biblical evangelism (such as anger and hostility) can easily resurface during the planting stage. Yes, a coworker may have grown to trust us, but our planting may remind him of an earlier, unpleasant experience with a Christian he couldn't trust—causing old emotions of doubt and rejection to resurface. When they do, recognize and appreciate these emotions—and don't take it personally.

TELLING YOUR STORY

One of the most compelling ways to convey spiritual truth and talk about the gospel message with your coworkers and friends is to recount the events of how you came to know Jesus and how knowing him has enriched your own and your family's lives. The apostle John wrote, "We proclaim to you what we have seen and heard" (1 John 1:3). To tell someone what you have seen or experienced—that's what a witness does. Of course, you were not a witness to Jesus' life on earth, but you are a witness to what he's done and is doing in your life. No one knows your story better than you. And no one can tell it quite like you can to your friends and coworkers.

Once Barb and I (Walt) were on a train slowly moving through the high passes of the Canadian Rockies. On this trip I was speaking to a group of professionals each morning and evening. We spent our days on the train—where we could survey the spectacular scenery. One afternoon I was on the observation deck with a man named Barry. "Man, what beautiful scenery," he remarked. "Almost makes you think there could be a God."

I silently nodded, in my mind asking God how I should respond. After a moment I asked, "If there is a God, how do you think he would try to communicate with us?"

"Good question," my trainmate responded. "Maybe through our hearts, or maybe through circumstances." He paused. "Maybe through ministers."

"How about through nature?" I inquired.

He smiled. "Obviously," he whispered, as we stared out at the mountains.

"In the Bible," I said, "it says that God's invisible qualities have been clearly seen in what he created."

He turned to look at me. "Is that what it says?"

"Yep," I replied, "that and a whole lot more."

He turned back toward the mountains—to think. I stood quietly by, taking time to pray that the Lord would use this faith flag. He did.

Later that afternoon, Barry approached me. "Mind if I sit?" he asked. I gestured at him to sit. "I know you know a lot about business and medicine," he said, "but how'd you learn so much about the Bible?"

I said, "Barry, do you mind if I tell you a story?"

He nodded his assent, and I stepped through the open door he'd given me. For the next five minutes I told him my personal story of faith—the story of the many needs I'd had before I committed my life to Jesus, of how I'd come to know and understand who Jesus is and how my life had been changed since I began to trust and follow him day by day. I ended by asking, "Does that make sense?"

He nodded. "I need to think about it a little bit." He got up and walked away, and I was left to pray and to leave the results to God.

That evening he came up after supper, and we spoke again. I took a moment to check his understanding of what I had said and was pleased to find that he had grasped most of it. With his permission, I clarified a couple of points. Our conversation continued throughout the trip, as well as in the months since. Barry doesn't have a personal relationship with God—yet—but he certainly understands the gospel. He wasn't ready to make a decision, but he now knows how. This is what the planting phase is all about.

A BIBLICAL EXAMPLE

When Paul stood before King Agrippa (Acts 26), he spoke simply and clearly about how he had come to know Jesus and how Jesus had dramatically changed his life. In his answer to Agrippa, Paul provides an excellent model for the telling of our personal faith stories. As we might expect, he uses an organized and logical approach, beginning with a brief introduction (verses 2–3), then sharing about his life *before* he met Jesus (verses 4–11), *how* he met Jesus (verses 12–18), and his life *after* meeting Jesus (verses 19–22a).

Paul delivered his testimony before the king and his court in a natural and conversational tone. What's more, it probably took only three or four minutes to tell. While Paul's language may be too "religious" to use with many nonbelievers today, the essence of his story and his way of telling it are as fresh and powerful in our day as they were almost two thousand years ago.

AN IMPORTANT RECOMMENDATION

We recommend that every follower of Jesus develop his or her own personal faith story. It's a good idea to outline it or write it out in full, and then share it with mature Christians. Ask them to critique your testimony and to help you make it more effective. Make sure they help you spot and eliminate confusing religious jargon.

We do *not* recommend, though, that you memorize your testimony and learn to give it verbatim. The whole purpose of writing and rehearsing your story is to avoid religious jargon, which can raise unnecessary obstacles.

As you prepare to develop your faith story, begin with prayer. Ask God for wisdom about how to shape and share your story. Be open to all suggestions made by mature Christians—especially those you know are comfortable spending time with and conversing with nonbelievers. It is critical to set aside time for prayer and preparation for this task. Many of the men and women that I (Walt) have mentored say that the work they put into preparing their personal faith stories was one of the most fruitful exercises of their early discipleship—and the telling of faith stories one of the most usable tools in biblical evangelism.

Don't expect to write out your faith story in one night. It takes the average person a number of drafts. The more complex your story, the more work it will require. Some stories are especially difficult to tell, and most have to be condensed so that they'll communicate effectively.

Your story, of course, can be tailored to just about any type of audience and length. But for the purposes of expressing grace in the workplace, we suggest you shape your testimony so that it is (1) understandable by a nonbeliever, (2) designed for telling either in a small group or one-on-one, and (3) intended to open a spiritual door for further discussion.

DEVELOPING YOUR OWN STORY

Keep the following principles in mind as you prepare to write the first draft of your testimony:

Principle 1: Use Conversational Language

Avoid a formal tone. What you write should *not* sound like a term paper. Your language should be natural and comfortable to read and to listen to.

*Jean, I remember feeling the same way when I was younger. My
life just didn't have any zest or zing. I was busy at work, but it just
didn't bring me any joy or satisfaction.*

Principle 2: Tell a Story – Don't Preach

Use "I" and "me," not "you" or "you should" or "you will."
Your story needs to be about *you* (not "them") and should be warm
and personal, pleasant and relaxed.

*There were so many things I had done wrong—some I felt par-
ticularly guilty about. But there was no way I could turn the hands of
the clock back, no way to undo what I had done.*

Principle 3: Be General; Avoid Using Too Many Specifics

Avoid the names of pastors or churches or Christian groups or
denominations—any of which could raise an obstacle. Try to avoid
specific dates, ages, or locations.

*I had lunch with a friend one day. I knew that he had a personal
relationship with God. I was wondering about that, and he told me.
He explained what the Bible had to say about my loneliness and my
lack of satisfaction with life and work.*

Principle 4: Include Human Interest
or a Humorous Touch

When you tell a story that touches real life and makes someone
smile or laugh, it reduces tension and increases attention. Human
interest draws people in, and humor is disarming—allowing your
coworker to drop his or her defenses. Net effect? It lowers obstacles.

*My friend suggested I take my Bible and read John. I was con-
fused. Why did I have to take the Bible into the bathroom to read?
He explained to me that John was a book in the Bible, and I could
read it anywhere I wanted.*

Principle 5: Use Word Pictures

Instead of saying, "My pastor shared the gospel with me over
lunch," why not help your friend "see" in the mind's eye what you

saw? If you've ever eaten in a cafeteria, chances are your mind's eye can picture this scene. Maybe you can even hear the noises around you:

> We met in the cafeteria at work one summer day. It was really hot, and the cafeteria was busy as usual—with lots of laughter and chatter all around us—but my mind was focused on what he was sharing with me.

Principle 6: Use Your Story as an Opportunity to Briefly Explain the Gospel

Telling your story can lead in a natural, unforced way to a brief explanation of the gospel that can plant a seed in your hearer's heart.

> My friend explained that I was just like every other human—I had done so many wrong things and these dishonest actions put me in a position where I was separated from God. I did not and could not have a personal relationship with him. Because he is holy and just, he could only judge me for all my wrongs. I want to tell you, if what he was telling me was true, it was pretty bad news. But then, almost as if he read my mind, he told me that there was some really good news—that this God also deeply loved me and because of his love he had sent Jesus—his Son—to live a perfect life where he did no wrong and to die on the cross for all my wrongdoing. His death paid the penalty that God demanded for my wrongs. My friend told me I couldn't earn this and I'd never deserve it. It was simply a free gift from God. If I would accept this gift and learn to trust and obey God day by day, then he could and would forgive all my wrong, and life could begin again—with him and me having a personal relationship and, best of all, me being given love, joy, peace, patience, kindness, goodness, faithfulness, gentleness, and self-control. I tell you, those were some of the things I desperately needed in my life.

When you give the basics of the gospel in your story, your story is very unlikely to threaten your listener. If possible, and if it feels natural to you, try to cover the basic points of the gospel message, points summarized in the seven questions in chapter 10 (pages 155–56).

Principle 7: Explain How God Is Meeting Your Deepest Inner Needs

Avoid communicating the impression that when you trust Jesus all the uncertainty in your daily life goes away, that becoming a Christian solves every problem, or that the Christian life is free from struggle. After all, you know that these impressions are not true. You can and should communicate that Christians can possess a joy, a peace, a hope, a satisfaction, that non-Christians cannot experience.

Since I began my personal relationship with God, my problems haven't gone away. Like you, I have to deal with the daily struggles and hassles of life. But what this relationship has given me is a peace and a deep satisfaction with life. I'm a lot better able to cope with disappointments and problems. Best of all, I know for a fact that when I face death, I'll spend eternity with my Creator.

STARTING A BIBLE STUDY

When you discover that the hearts of several persons are cultivated to the point where they could begin to receive biblical truth, consider starting a Bible study. This may be one of the most effective ways to help people discover the truth for themselves in a supportive atmosphere. The great thing is that you don't need to be a top-notch Bible scholar to lead it. Your main technique can be *asking* questions—not necessarily answering questions—to stimulate nonbelievers to seek answers themselves. You are not the theological expert, just a fellow traveler on the same road of discovering more about who Jesus is and what God is teaching and doing for you.

In moments when you feel inadequate, remember that the real force for change is in Scripture itself, not in a teacher's instruction. Let the Word of God speak for itself. If the group gets stuck on a tough question or issue you can't negotiate, get help from your pastor or a teacher you respect.

Over the course of time, we've learned that a Bible study works best in an atmosphere that is (1) fun and relaxed, (2) free of religious jargon, and (3) nonthreatening. It's usually best to avoid such things as asking a group member to read aloud (just have people read the passage silently), giving your opinion on something the Bible doesn't address, and going into great depth of teaching.

Because we're passionate about wanting people to fall in love with Jesus, we'd suggest a study of one of the four gospels. Focus more on what Matthew, Mark, Luke, or John thinks than on what the participants think. Help people find their way to Jesus by asking additional questions—and try wherever possible to answer their questions from the Bible itself. If you don't know an answer, say so.

If you do study a gospel, focus on these questions: (1) Who is Jesus? (2) What does the biblical writer believe about Jesus? (3) What does the author say about Jesus (or about the subject being studied)? You may want to begin with a launching question such as, "What is John referring to when he speaks of 'the Word' in his opening verses?" Use these kinds of guiding questions to keep the discussion moving:

- Why do you think he said that?
- What do you think he was getting at?
- What else do you see?
- What do you mean by that?
- Why do you say that? How did you arrive at that conclusion?
- Where did we see this same idea before?
- How does this affect you? How can you use this information this week?

As the session ends, invite people to summarize the discussion or the section being studied. You might ask something like this: (1) How would you summarize the main idea of this paragraph? or (2) How would you say this in your own words?

Although we love studying Jesus' story with nonbelievers, I (Bill) have a friend who often uses the book of Proverbs in his study groups. Its wisdom is very applicable to the workplace and may convince someone that he or she just can't ignore the Bible as being merely ancient history.

No matter where you start, the Word of God is powerful. God will speak through it to anyone who comes with a seeker's heart. Dr. Bob Snyder, when ministering in Budapest, met an Algerian man who had come to Jesus from Islam by reading the Bible. He had begun in the book of Proverbs. When he came to Proverbs 3:5–6 ("Trust in the LORD with all your heart and lean not on your own understanding; in all your ways acknowledge him, and he will make your paths straight"), he recognized this could only be the word of God. From there, he went on to discover, love, and trust Jesus—not as someone who was a great Islamic prophet but as God's Son, his own Savior and Lord.

THE BOTTOM LINE									

As hearts begin to soften, God will create a desire in people to discuss spiritual realities that will create a heart-readiness for biblical truth.

10

THE WHOLE TRUTH

Brent's wife had suddenly decided to walk away from the marriage and their two young girls. He came to church with his coworker Rob, looking for answers to why his life was falling apart. His heart was already under cultivation from his agonizing circumstances and also through Rob's godly influence. Rob and his wife had been there for Brent when his daughter had gotten sick, and they had opened their home to Brent's kids when he had to be out of town on business. They had had him over regularly for meals, often talking well into the night about his questions about Jesus and Christianity, planting spiritual truth.

At Rob's request, I (Bill) had joined a team of people praying for Brent's salvation, and in time I began a friendship with him. We met for lunch once a month or so. After talking about the tough times in the oil industry, we got around to spiritual questions. Sometimes I couldn't tell whether he just wanted a second opinion for an argument he was having with Rob or whether he was truly seeking God.

I hadn't talked with Brent for several weeks when he called and suggested lunch. He wanted to buy me "the best steak in town." I have to admit I was skeptical when we walked into a Chinese restaurant, but it turned out to be the best steak I had eaten in years. As good as the steak was, though, he had another agenda. We were soon into a conversation about guilt, with which he was struggling to no small degree.

As the server cleared the table, I decided it was time to explain the gospel to Brent. I grabbed a paper napkin and illustrated how he could experience forgiveness through Jesus. I sketched a simple bridge diagram (see page 162) to show what Jesus had done for us through his crucifixion and resurrection.

Brent had grown up in a nominally Christian family, but his experience with God and the church had majored in guilt and condemnation. I felt I needed to stress the freeness of God's offer. He longed for a relationship with God but just couldn't accept the fact that he didn't have to *do* something to earn God's love. He balked at God's graciousness.

As we got up to leave, Brent said, "I'm going to really think about this," and then he opened his fortune cookie. The fortune inside read, "Beware of strangers bearing free gifts." We both laughed, but inside I cringed. How difficult it is for people to accept eternal life as a free gift! And how vigilant Satan's forces are, ready to snatch the word—the seed—right out of a person's heart the moment it is planted.

As I stared at Brent's fortune, which I kept as a reminder, I thought of Jesus' explanation of his parable of the sower: "When anyone hears the message about the kingdom and does not understand it, the evil one comes and snatches away what was sown in his heart. This is the seed sown along the path" (Matthew 13:19).

That day I saw the forces of evil in plain sight—this fortune cookie was no coincidence. I prayed and wondered if these forces would be able to snatch away the truth from Brent's heart. But I shouldn't have doubted the power of the seed sown in a *cultivated* heart. The danger Jesus points out is for the seed of his word that falls on an uncultivated heart. A week later, as we sat on a downtown park bench, Brent trusted Jesus as his Savior.

I've come to believe that if Brent's heart hadn't been cultivated by circumstances, by hours of observing the lives of godly coworkers and receiving their love, and by the planting that occurred during hours of conversation about his spiritual questions, it wouldn't have mattered how clearly and persuasively the gospel was presented that day. The "birds" would have had a feast.

GETTING TO THE GOOD NEWS

Timing is critical in the planting stage. Just as generations ago farmers planted religiously by the *Farmer's Almanac*, we need to take great care in planting God's truth by the Spirit's leading.

This doesn't mean that we adopt fancy, sophisticated techniques to improve our timing. Rather, we must increase our sensitivity to what God's Spirit is doing in our coworkers' lives.

Press the gospel too soon and the word falls on hard, dry ground. But we must take care to avoid the opposite problem. If the time is right and a person's heart is ready but we fail to recognize the open door or feel awkward about presenting the gospel, we miss an opportunity to plant in a well-cultivated heart.

How do we gently and respectfully steer a conversation toward a presentation of the gospel message? We do it in part by nudging a conversation without trying to control it. Here are some examples of statements and questions to consider using as a transition to discuss spiritual truth. Clearly they assume an existing relationship of some sort.

> *Fred, we've never had a chance to talk about your religious background. I'm curious, do you have an interest in spiritual matters?*

(Let the other person talk.)

> *Sandy, I'd like the opportunity sometime to share some principles with you that may help you understand what it means to establish a personal relationship with Jesus.*

(Let the other person talk.)

> *Has anyone ever taken a Bible and shown you how you can know for sure that you have a relationship with God? I'd love to do that sometime, but only if you're interested.*

(Wait for response.)

> *Has anyone ever taken a Bible and shown you how you can experience God's love and forgiveness? I'd love to do that sometime, if that's OK with you.*

(Let her express her interest level.)

> *Has anyone ever shown you what God says in the Bible about how you can have a personal, life-changing relationship with him?*

(If yes, follow with the next question.)

If by only using one short verse from the Bible I could show you most of the basics taught in all sixty-six books of the Bible, would you be interested?

(Let him respond. If he says yes, determine if the time and place are right; if not, schedule a time—perhaps over lunch at some point during the next few days. If he declines an opportunity to talk further, don't look hurt or dismayed. This isn't about you but about God and his timing. Thank him for giving you the chance to ask him; if it seems right, follow up with a kindly worded reminder to connect with you if he ever wants to talk about this.)

There are times in the planting process when the diagnostic questions below, asked in love, could be appropriate. But we urge discretion, because these questions, asked at the wrong time or in the wrong way, can raise barriers. Remember, we're following

---

DIAGNOSTIC QUESTIONS
(use with extreme caution and sensitivity)

Evangelism Explosion, probably the most widely taught evangelism training program, uses the following questions to establish where a person is spiritually—in other words, to diagnose a person's spiritual health. (We rarely use these questions, but if you have a solid relationship with someone, asking them may prove helpful.)

1. Have you come to a place in your life where you know for certain that if you were to die today, you would go to heaven?
2. Suppose you were to die tonight and stand before God, and he were to ask you, "Why should I let you into heaven?" What would you say to him?

If a person wants to understand how to have a relationship with God, I sometimes use a modified form of these questions: If you were to stand before God right now and he were to ask you, "Why should I let you into heaven?" what would you say?

God's agenda, not our own. Find out what God is doing before you attempt to pick green fruit with questions such as these:

EXPLAINING THE GOSPEL MESSAGE

Even as we acknowledge that there are many steps that precede a gospel presentation, workplace grace requires ultimately that we know how to present the gospel message clearly and concisely. We have a message from God to pass on when the time is right:

> I [Paul] want to remind you of the gospel I preached to you, which you received and on which you have taken your stand. By this gospel you are saved, if you hold firmly to the word I preached to you. Otherwise, you have believed in vain.
>
> For what I received I passed on to you as of first importance: that Christ died for our sins according to the Scriptures, that he was buried, that he was raised on the third day according to the Scriptures, and that he appeared to Peter, and then to the Twelve.
>
> 1 Corinthians 15:1–5

In this book we have de-emphasized harvesting, but only that we may emphasize cultivation, the importance of which is typically underrated. Nevertheless, cultivation that doesn't have the harvest in mind is shortsighted if not misguided. People need to see the gospel in your life, but at an appropriate point they also need to understand the details of the gospel message if they are to come to believe in Jesus and receive eternal life:

> How, then, can they call on the one they have not believed in? And how can they believe in the one of whom they have not heard? And how can they hear without someone preaching to them?...
>
> Consequently, faith comes from hearing the message, and the message is heard through the word of Christ.
>
> Romans 10:14, 17

In Colossians 4:3–4, Paul asked the believers to pray for two things regarding his communication of the gospel. After asking them to pray for an open door—an opportunity to speak—he requests, "Pray that I may proclaim [the mystery of Christ] clearly, as I should." Clarity isn't something for which we just pray; it is something we prepare for as well by learning to communicate the gospel succinctly so that others come to understand that eternal life is by grace alone, through faith alone, in Christ alone.

What would the gospel, presented clearly, look like? Although one could say there are as many ways to present the message as there are people, we believe that a presentation of the gospel ought to help a person answer seven basic questions:

1. WHO IS GOD?

The story begins with God, not with humans, so it's important for a person to know something about God. He is the personal, eternal, all-powerful, all-knowing, ever-present, supremely great spiritual being who created the heavens and the earth. He is absolute perfection and beauty. He is the source of meaning and love. Without him, there is no life or love. God has revealed himself as one, true, eternal God in three persons (Trinity) — Father, Son, and Holy Spirit.

2. WHO ARE WE?

All individuals need to have a grasp of who we are in the bigger story. We were created by God to rule the world and experience a perfect relationship with God and with one another. We rebelled, however, making a choice as a race to please ourselves rather than to follow God's ways, thus plunging the entire world and ourselves into the pain, insecurity, confusion, and powerlessness resulting from living apart from God, who is the source of life. We've missed God's mark, having been disobedient in our actions and attitudes. We cannot even live up to our own standards, much less to God's. As a result, we live separated from God and under judgment, unable to free ourselves from our bondage to wrongdoing.

3. WHO IS JESUS?

People need to see that Jesus is able to do something about their problems. He is the divine Son of God (second person of the Trinity), Lord of the universe, and source of eternal life. He is eternal and fully God. He loves men and women so much that he left heaven to come to earth—taking on human nature—to live, die, and be resurrected so he could restore his original purpose for us.

4. WHAT DID JESUS DO?

What we couldn't do for ourselves, Jesus did for us. In an act of love and grace, he chose to die in our place. Because he is true God and at the same time truly human and truly righteous, he was able to take the penalty of our sin—the sentence of death—on himself. By doing so, he made forgiveness, a relationship with God, and eternal life possible. His life restores our lives.

5. WHAT CAN WE NOT DO?

We are powerless to change the way we are. We can't earn our pardon or free ourselves from the sentence of death by good deeds, by faith plus good deeds, or by faith plus our good intentions to change our lives.

6. WHAT DO WE HAVE TO DO?

All we *have* to do is also the only thing we *can* do. And that is to receive Jesus, God's eternal Son, as our own Savior by faith, depending totally on him as the only basis for our relationship with God.

7. WHAT DOES GOD PROMISE TO THOSE WHO BELIEVE?

God promises to forgive all our wrongdoings, to give us eternal life, to make us new, to make us part of his family, to make his home in our hearts, and to love us unconditionally. He doesn't promise to remove our problems, but he does promise to strengthen us as we face our problems. And he grants us the power to become everything we were designed to be—the power to live lives overflowing with meaning and purpose.

THE MESSAGE IN A VERSE

In your explanation of the gospel message, you may not always cover all seven questions, but it is important for you to be able to clearly communicate the essence of this message in an understandable way if someone asks you to explain "the reason for the hope that you have" (1 Peter 3:15).

While gospel tracts have their place in gospel communication, we think it's more natural and comfortable to create your own tract, using an approach like the one described below. You can create this tract anywhere, using just a scrap of paper or a napkin to tell the story of what Jesus has done. Health care professionals who have taken "The Saline Solution" course have appreciated the succinctness and clarity of this method. The hardest part may be memorizing Romans 6:23: "For the wages of sin is death, but the gift of God is eternal life in Christ Jesus our Lord." Once you've memorized it, you've got the outline of your presentation. You can spend as little as five minutes on the basics, or you can expand the discussion as time and the interest of your listener allow.

A person who is ready to hear the Good News often asks questions that reveal an openness to spiritual things. It's at this point in your relationship that you could ask: "If I could show you one verse from the Bible that explains the basic message of all sixty-six books of the Bible at one time, would you be interested in hearing about it?" If a person's heart is cultivated, he or she usually responds positively.

Begin by writing out Romans 6:23. Draw a box around the word *wages*, and then rewrite *wages* in the diagram. (Be sure to keep in mind that asking questions and engaging a person along the way is much more effective than a monologue. From your listener's responses, you can determine if he or she is still with you.)

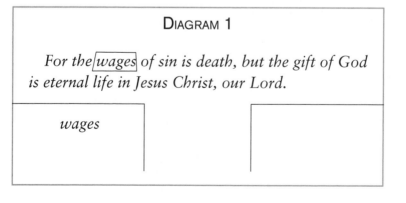

DIAGRAM 1

For the ⃞wages⃞ of sin is death, but the gift of God is eternal life in Jesus Christ, our Lord.

wages

Ask questions such as "What concept comes to mind when I use the word *wages*?" "What does it mean to you to receive wages?" or "What happens if you don't get paid for what you do? Is that just or right?" From your listener's impressions, you'll learn more about his or her belief system.

Now go back to the verse and draw a box around the word *sin*. Right below the word *wages* on the diagram, write the word *sin*. Ask a question such as "What does the word *sin* mean to you?" Don't comment on the appropriateness of the answer; just listen. Don't argue or tell him he's wrong. When he's finished, simply explain that when the Bible uses the word *sin*, it means more than breaking some-body's religious rules. It describes human beings' failure to follow God, our attempts to make other things more important than God, our desire to run our own lives.

Admit your own failure: "I regularly fall short of what I want to be—and, more important, what God wants me to be." Explain that the word *sin* literally means "to fall short, to miss the mark." Many today think of sin as a set of behaviors defined by religious people—a measure someone uses to judge others who are misbehaving. The truth you want to convey is that what matters is not a person's stan-dards but *God*'s standards. Sin isn't about rules; it's about a relation-ship—an improper relationship with the Creator of the universe. We sin when we substitute anything else as the highest priority in our lives.

Before going further, you may want to confess your own discomfort from not having always put God first in your life. Then maybe you'd say, "Sam, you're a great guy, but I'm guessing you don't think you've lived a perfect life either. Have you always been pleased with what you do? What do you think God thinks?" Give him time to respond.

Ask questions with friendly sensitivity. As you acknowledge your own struggle with sin, your listener is less likely to feel judged. People instinctively know they haven't met God's standard. We're all in the same boat when it comes to this accusation. Before going on, get some agreement that *everyone sins*. Then it's time to proceed to the bad news.

Begin this next step by saying, "If we fall short, we've got a wage coming. And the Bible says the wages of sin is death." Put a box around the word *death* and write it below the word *sin* on the diagram. Then ask, "What comes to mind when you hear the word *death*?" or "Is death a scary thing to think about for you?" Briefly explain that the Bible talks not just about physical death (separation from the body) but also about spiritual death (separation from God, who is the source of life). Draw any other parallels between spiritual and physical death that come to mind and explain that physical death is the result of spiritual death. Then you may want to ask, "How do you feel when God says that the wages of sin is separation from him? That's pretty bad news, isn't it?"

Now explain that the canyon you've drawn represents a gulf between the first three words on the left side of the paper and words you'll write on the other side. Explain that "sin separates us from life and puts a big gulf between us and God." Box the word *God* in the verse and write it on the right side of the diagram. Make the observation that "according to the Bible, this separation would have lasted forever, except for the fact that God did something for us we couldn't do for ourselves." Draw a box around the word *but* in the verse and put it at the bottom of the canyon. "This *but* tells us there is good news ahead!"

DIAGRAM 2

For the ⟨*wages*⟩ *of* ⟨*sin*⟩ *is* ⟨*death*⟩ ⟨*but*⟩ *the gift of* ⟨*God*⟩ *is eternal life in Jesus Christ, our Lord.*

wages *sin* *death*	*but*	God

Put a box around the word *gift* in the verse and write it down on the right side of the diagram below the word *God*. Ask questions about gifts: "What's a gift? If you buy something, is it a gift? Can you earn a gift? If you earn a gift, is it really a gift?" You'll then be able to explain that something earned or bought is a wage or a purchase, not a gift. A true gift is free—no strings attached, no conditions. The motivation of the gift is internal in the giver, not external in the receiver. If something is given with a price or a condition, it is not a gift. Many of your listeners will agree with you, but some may want to argue that some gifts have strings attached. If so, don't argue. Merely explain that the Greek word Paul uses here means "free."

Then ask something like this: "When does a gift become a gift?" You could do an object lesson here. Pick up a pen or some object near you and hand it to your listener. "Here, this is a gift, please take it." When she takes it from you, say, "When did the gift become yours? When I gave it or when you took it?" (Clearly it became a gift when she took it.)

Pointing to the words on the diagram, say, "God has a gift he wants to give us." You may want to ask the questions "What will this gift cost us?" and "When does it become ours?" If your listener says that it costs us nothing, you know she got the point.

It's always helpful to talk about the person's concept of God. "Who is God to you?" "What's your feeling about God?" "Where did you get those feelings?" Some people see God as harsh and exacting; some see him as loving and lenient. Explain that the Bible tells us that God is both a just Judge and a loving Father. In the case of someone arguing a point, you may note that different people have all kinds of opinions about a specific person. You can even think you know someone and then discover an entirely different side. (If you have a story about judging someone on an initial impression, only to find out later that you lacked the whole picture, this is a good time to tell it.) Go on to say, "You know, you can learn a lot about someone by listening to that person and especially by watching how that person acts. But I think the only way we really know someone else is if that person genuinely opens his or her heart up to us. You may disagree, but I believe God's done that in the Bible."

If your listener seems uncomfortable, you may say, "I sense you're struggling with this. We can talk about this later if you want to." But think about leaving a challenge such as this: "I wonder if you're willing to see if God will reveal himself to you. The Bible tells us we can see God in Jesus, so would you be willing to read the gospel of Luke [or pick your favorite gospel] and see what happens and get back to me."[1]

If, on the other hand, your listener is still tracking with you, draw a box around the words *eternal life* and write the words below the word *gift*. Say something like this: "This is the good news: The gift that God offers is eternal life." Again, get feedback on what this means to her. Affirm her when she's on track. Explain that eternal life is more than a home in heaven; it is a relationship with God in his family that starts the moment we receive his gift. The life we receive from him is *his* life, and this changes our whole identity from here to all eternity. God offers to forgive our wrongdoings and let us begin again. He offers to make us new on the inside—to change us from the inside out and make it possible for us to be what we were created to be. He gives us the freedom to say no to what we know is wrong and yes to what we know is right. He offers a relationship with himself—a relationship that meets the deepest longings of our heart the way no earthly person, thing, or experience can.

Be sure to center your conversation on what the Bible has to say. Avoid phrases such as "I think" or "I believe." What's important here is what *God* says. It's God's Word, not our opinions, that has power. Remember that "the word of God is living and active. Sharper than any double-edged sword, it penetrates even to dividing soul and spirit, joints and marrow; it judges the thoughts and attitudes of the heart" (Hebrews 4:12).

Before you go to the next step, briefly summarize: "So we've got all men and women (including you and me) starting out over here, separated from God because of sin. And over here we've got God, who has life and wants to give it to us." Explain how the character of God fits here. "Because God is a righteous judge, the gulf exists. He can't just ignore what men and women have done to themselves and his creation. He told us that failing to follow him and trying to run our own lives would be disastrous. And that's why we're over here wallowing in this mess."

It may also be helpful to explain the following concepts. God is doing three things by bringing judgment on us: (1) He's keeping his word and showing us that he is just. (2) He's treating us with respect, allowing us to make our own choices and experience the consequences of going our own way. (3) Through the pain we feel in the world as a result of humanity's choices he gives us a wake-up call, telling us that something is terribly wrong and that somebody needs to do something before it's too late.

Then ask the question, "If people who had chosen to run their own lives wanted a solution to their relationship with God, where do you think they would look?" Try to get your listener to see that humans would look to themselves. It's what most world religions have in common—a plan for humans to find their way back to God. While the formula differs from religion to religion, it's usually *us* who develop a plan to get ourselves back to where we belong. The formula in Islam is utter submission and obedience to Allah. The formula in most Eastern religions involves discipline and denial of human passions so they won't control us. Ancestor worship in Chinese, Korean, and Japanese cultures involves living a worthy life and bringing honor to your family. Animism in its various forms usually involves formulas to keep evil spirits of local deities placated or put in a position where they're compelled to bless you. This natural inclination to do it ourselves is so strong that it can even work its way into the mind-sets of some Christians, who think that by going to church or doing good deeds they can earn God's favor.

If you'd rather not go into such detail, simply say, "Religion is humanity's best attempt to please God—to bridge this gap through self-effort. But if what we've said is true, there's nothing anyone can do that is enough to bridge the gulf. You can't buy it; you can't earn it. God isn't impressed by what we can do. But he *is* interested in a personal relationship with each person. We cannot get to him, but because he loves us so much, he has come to us."

Now put a box around the words *Christ Jesus our Lord* in the verse and draw a cross bridging the chasm. Write *Christ Jesus Lord* in the cross. This is what your diagram should look like now.

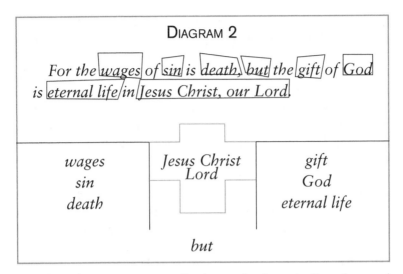

Take a few moments to talk about who Jesus is. Box the word *Jesus* in the verse. Jesus, the divine Son of God, took on human flesh and lived on earth as a human being. He got tired, hungry, thirsty, sweaty, angry, sad, and joyful—just as we all do. He was like us in every way, except for one thing: He never sinned; he never turned away from God and tried to run his own life as a human.

But Jesus is more than a human. Draw a box around *Lord* in the verse. Jesus is God. The Bible declares it, and the Holy Spirit produces faith in our hearts to believe it. Everywhere Jesus went in a world of pain, hurt, and rejection, he demonstrated that he was the divine Son of God. People were able to experience God in a new way because Jesus was fully human as well as fully divine. Because he was God, he could not remain in the grave. He arose and now reigns in heaven at the right hand of the Father.

Jesus had a mission. Draw a box around *Christ* in the verse. Christ means "anointed one." God the Father anointed Jesus to come to earth to willingly die for us. Even though he never sinned, he died because of sin—our sin—in our place. He took the consequences of our sin on himself. He could die for us because he was truly human. He could offer himself as a substitute for every man, woman, and child who would ever live because he was also true

God and truly righteous. So because of who he is—100 percent divine and 100 percent human—he was able to offer himself as a full, perfect, and sufficient substitute for the sins of the world. God accepted Jesus' sacrifice and now offers the benefits of Jesus' death, resurrection, and ascension to everyone who will believe in him. Here is where several other verses are helpful in explaining how we receive the gift (John 1:12–13; John 3:1–8, 16–18; Romans 3:22–28). Memorize them or mark them in your Bible so you can find them quickly.

To bring the gospel presentation to a conclusion, you may want to ask, "What do you think about all this? Do you need some time to think about it? Can you think of anything that would keep you from making a decision to trust Jesus and become his follower?" Be willing to say, "Take your time. This is an important decision." Offer the person the drawing, and ask if he or she wants to talk further.

THE BEST METHOD

Creating your own tract is one of many ways to communicate the gospel. Telling your own story of how you came to faith, as discussed in chapter 9, is another. One of the most interesting presentations is found in Rick Richardson's book *Evangelism Outside the Box*. It's an excellent resource on talking about spiritual subjects with young people in the postmodern era. He calls his method of presenting the gospel "Inviting People into the Circle of Belonging."[2] George Barna's approach, called "Socratic Evangelism,"[3] is also worth studying.

The "best method," in the end, is the one that feels comfortable to you, that you're willing to use, and that fits the situation. There is one message, but there is no one right way to present it. Whatever method you choose, here are a few guidelines to consider:

LEARN THE BASICS

According to George Barna, most American Christians can't explain the facts about the core truths of the Christian faith or why they are Christians.[4] We place a high value on being well grounded in Scripture and in the basics of the Christian faith. Every Christian needs to follow Jesus' teaching—which means we must know what the Bible says. It will be difficult to communicate the Bible's truths to others if you haven't learned them yourself.

If colleagues ask questions you can't answer, immerse yourself in God's Word to discover answers. Mark in your Bible the key verses that teach what you're declaring about the gospel. Whatever method you choose to communicate the gospel, you would do well to memorize—or be able to quickly find—the following verses (in addition to the ones mentioned above) that are basic to the gospel message:

Our sin and its consequences:

"We all, like sheep, have gone astray, each of us has turned to his own way; and the LORD has laid on him the iniquity of us all" (Isaiah 53:6).

Jesus' sacrifice:

"But God demonstrates his own love for us in this: While we were still sinners, Christ died for us" (Romans 5:8).

"For Christ died for sins once for all, the righteous for the unrighteous, to bring you to God" (1 Peter 3:18).

"As far as the east is from the west, so far has [the Lord] removed our transgressions from us" (Psalm 103:12).

Receiving Jesus and eternal life:

"And this is the testimony: God has given us eternal life, and this life is in his Son. He who has the Son has life; he who does not have the Son of God does not have life. I write these things to you who believe in the name of the Son of God so that you may know that you have eternal life" (1 John 5:11–13).

"For I am convinced that neither death nor life, neither angels nor demons, neither the present nor the future, nor any powers, neither height nor depth, nor anything else in all creation, will be able to separate us from the love of God that is in Christ Jesus our Lord" (Romans 8:38–39).

If you memorize these verses, you'll always have the biblical truth ready for an unplanned discussion when you don't have a Bible handy. If you use the Romans 6:23 outline, it's helpful to write these

166 • Workplace Grace

references on that piece of paper for the person to look up later. If he or she doesn't have a Bible, you can refer to a Bible website such as biblegateway.com, where someone can look up verses in nineteen languages and eleven versions and even read a commentary.

Practice Your Presentation

One reason Christians sometimes hesitate to share their faith is because it seems awkward. Some of this hesitation is natural; some comes from not being prepared. A great way to gain confidence is to practice. Learn the outline of the presentation you're choosing. Memorize the verses you want to use (or know where to find them in your Bible), and find a trustworthy person with whom you can practice. We suggest a good Christian friend for your first attempt. Have someone listen as you go all the way through. Then ask him or her for suggestions for improvement. Make the changes as you repeat the presentation; feel free to have the listener interact with you along the way.

If you have a good friend who is a nonbeliever and you want good feedback, ask him or her to listen to your presentation. Was anything unclear? Did I use confusing words? After all, you never know what can come of this experience.

Stay Ready

Paul exhorted Timothy to "be prepared in season and out of season" (2 Timothy 4:2). Peter urged his readers to "always be prepared to give an answer to everyone who asks you to give the reason for the hope that you have" (1 Peter 3:15). We never know when an open door for the gospel will present itself.

The Joy of the Harvest

In John 4 when the disciples returned from the Samaritan market with lunch for themselves and Jesus, they were preoccupied with getting food in their stomachs. But etiquette prevented them from eating before their rabbi, so they pleaded with him to eat. Unfortunately for their stomachs, though, Jesus had something else on his mind. He had been at work cultivating and planting, and now it was time for the spiritual harvest. We don't want to pick green fruit, but neither do we want to neglect the harvest when the Lord of the harvest calls us into the fields.

Because God is always at work, whether we see him or not, we stay busy at the hard work of cultivating and planting, as well as preparing, practicing, and praying for opportunities to enter into the joy of the harvest of "the crop for eternal life" (John 4:36). On that day Jesus, the disciples, and the Samaritan woman all experienced the joy of seeing many other people place their faith in Jesus:

> Many of the Samaritans from that town believed in him because of the woman's testimony, "He told me everything I ever did." So when the Samaritans came to him, they urged him to stay with them, and he stayed two days. And because of his words many more became believers.
>
> John 4:39–41

Witnessing a new birth—whether physical or spiritual—is thrilling. And when you witness a new spiritual birth, know that all of heaven is rejoicing with you (see Luke 15:7, 10). Some of our most precious memories in life have to do with seeing friends, neighbors, and coworkers come to Jesus.

Like any farmer, the more you intentionally cultivate and plant, the more harvest you are likely to witness. Most of us who are not gifted in evangelism will spend more time cultivating and planting than we will harvesting. But it doesn't mean we miss the joy. Jesus said, "My food ... is to do the will of him who sent me and to finish his work" (John 4:34). The real joy is knowing that you are part of something bigger than yourself and that you are able to make an impact for the kingdom of God every day when you go to work.

THE BOTTOM LINE

People need to understand the details of the gospel message, so learn to give a clear, succinct explanation.

FACING OBJECTIONS

We hope that by now you're beginning to see your coworkers through a different prism—seeing them as God sees them—and observing the Holy Spirit at work in your workplace as you cultivate relationships and plant a little spiritual truth. If people have been responding, you've probably seen that spiritual realities can be disturbing to non-Christians. In the planting phase it's important that we know how to handle objections to the Christian faith.

How you respond to an objection is crucial, whether it relates to the gospel itself, to a particular tenet of the Christian faith, or to a delicate moral issue such as homosexuality, abortion, or physician-assisted suicide. Paul reminds us in Ephesians 4:15 that we are to speak the truth in love. It's not always easy to do so.

Lee is a follower of Jesus who worked as an on-air anchor for a national cable TV company. Jenny, a coworker who was not a believer, had worked as a production assistant for about a year. She had a passion for the plight of women who were less fortunate than she. This passion came to Lee's attention in a most unusual way.

Whenever he had an opportunity, Lee made it a point to speak with Jenny. He had also been praying for her openness to the gospel. After hearing Lee raise several faith flags and tell a few faith stories, Jenny seemed genuinely intrigued by his spiritual perspectives. At Lee's invitation, she had even attended a lunchtime Bible study at work.

One morning, after Lee had been up all night with a sick child, Jenny approached him with her usual buoyancy. "Hey, Lee, what do you think about this partial-birth abortion stuff Congress is debating?"

Lee *knew* instantly that this was a critical moment in the relationship. He gently and respectfully responded, "Well, Jenny, from my perspective, I think it's wrong. I believe that God sees a baby even at this stage as a valuable human life. It's a life we don't have the right to end." He paused and asked, "But, Jenny, I'm interested in what you think." He awaited her response.

Jenny's face turned red as she shot off a rapid-fire series of questions. "Well, Lee, what about the mother's rights? What if something is wrong with her baby? Doesn't she have any rights? Aren't her rights more important than a fetus? That's the problem with you Christian types; you love fetuses more than real people. What if she doesn't have a little Christian hubby or a little Christian home? What if she doesn't have any money? What about her, Lee, huh? What about her?"

Lee felt his blood pressure rising. The Bible's admonition to respond with gentleness and respect escaped him. Almost shouting at her, he answered, "Yeah, right! She has a right to have her baby partially delivered, jerked from the womb, have its skull pierced with no anesthesia at all, and have its brains sucked out into a jar? Do you think that's right?"

Jenny turned pale. As she stared at Lee, her eyes filled with tears and her lips quivered. She said, "I knew it. You're just like the rest of them."

When we tell this story at a workshop, the response is interesting. More times than not, before one of us delivers Jenny's final response, a few people spontaneously applaud to affirm Lee's stand against partial-birth abortion. Then when we report Jenny's response, a quiet hush settles over the audience.

Most people with any kind of heart realize that, although Lee's response may have been ethically solid, it wasn't very wise or compassionate. It instantly nullified much of the cultivating he had been doing. It severely damaged his relationship with Jenny, which, prior to this episode, was heading somewhere spiritually. Why Jenny asked the question about partial-birth abortion is anybody's guess, but we doubt she was looking for a contentious debate. She was certainly looking for a gentle and respectful answer from her Christian friend.

Jenny's past experiences had led her to conclude that all Christians were jerks, but Lee had been forcing her to rethink her conclusions. Chances are she wanted to talk about a difficult issue with someone with whom she felt safe, someone she respected. If Lee had responded differently, he might have been able to help Jenny gain a biblical perspective on the sanctity of life. Now there was little hope of that.

As stated earlier, we shouldn't be surprised when people who do not know Jesus Christ hold views that do not conform to the truth of Scripture. We should not pander to another person's arrogance, but non-Christians have every right to expect us to respond to their honest objections—even emotionally charged ones—with respect, gentleness, and thoughtfulness. This is what Jesus expects of those who represent him as they plant spiritual truth.

ON THE ATTACK?

When we feel strongly about what we believe, it's possible to get all fired up and seek "victory" at all costs. Let's remember that winning a battle is not as important as winning the war. If being right becomes more important than helping someone take steps toward understanding who Jesus is, we've lost sight of the main objective of the planting phase. James reminds us of the attitude we should seek to display in our relationships: "My dear brothers, take note of this: Everyone should be quick to listen, slow to speak and slow to become angry, for man's anger does not bring about the righteous life that God desires" (James 1:19–20).

What reaction would you expect from the following catch-phrase responses to objection?

- It's a proven fact that ...
- That's just the way it is.
- There's no question about ...
- Only fools believe ...
- *(In a dogmatic tone of voice)* The Bible says ...
- You don't know what you're talking about.
- That's ridiculous.
- Look at the evidence.
- That just doesn't fit the facts.
- You're not serious.
- Well, if you believe that, then ...
- There's just no evidence for ...
- Give me a break; that's been totally disproved.
- You're committing intellectual suicide.
- You're totally illogical.
- How can you even say that?

These responses can easily come across as a personal attack against someone and can cause him or her to become defensive and react emotionally. Remember that your coworker is not the enemy but is a captive of the Enemy. Your job is not to win an argument but to win a friend by demonstrating love as you seek to help someone find the truth.

Here are some ways to express disagreement that show respect while affirming the value of the individual and keeping the door open for further discussion:1

- I hear what you're saying, but it does raise a red flag for me.
- My perspective is a little different. Can I share it with you?
- Correct me if I'm wrong, but I see a conflict between ...
- I'm not piecing the facts together in the same way.
- That would make a lot of sense to me, but ...
- I agree with you concerning ..., but I see the issue differently.
- I'm not sure I agree. Could I hear that again?
- I was wondering, have you ever considered this perspective?
- Have you considered the evidence for ... ?
- Can I offer you another opinion?

SOCRATES, JESUS, AND LIEUTENANT COLUMBO

Christians can learn a lot about ways to get at the truth from one of our favorite TV characters, Columbo—a disheveled Los Angeles police lieutenant working in the homicide division. The character, portrayed by Peter Falk, didn't carry a gun. He drove a car "desperately in need of burial" and rarely took off his rumpled raincoat. But he always got his man—or woman.

To solve a case Columbo simply asked questions. He pondered the answers and then asked more questions. He was a gumshoe Socrates. He would get his leading suspect to declare what he or she thought happened, and then, over time, he'd whittle away at the logical inconsistencies. He wouldn't state that the person was wrong or accuse his suspect right off the bat. Refusing to act like a know-it-all, Colombo would play dumb, asking the person to explain what he didn't understand. In the end the truth inevitably surfaced.

SOCRATIC EVANGELISM

When it comes to objections to biblical truth, we have found that our Columbo-like questions can help a person recognize spiritual reality faster than our answers. Socrates wasn't the only one to lead people to the truth with a well-turned question. In fact, Jesus was the master of this art. He often used questions, as well as parables, to get his point across without directly engaging his opponents in a debate. Here are just a few of the many examples:

- One day, certain religious leaders who were trying to trap him asked, "Is it right to pay taxes to Caesar or not?" Jesus didn't answer the question. Instead he asked, "Whose portrait is this [on the coin]? And whose inscription?" (Matthew 22:17, 20).
- Some of the religious leaders zeroed in on Sabbath observance: "Is it lawful to heal on the Sabbath?" Jesus replied, "If any of you has a sheep and it falls into a pit on the Sabbath, will you not take hold of it and lift it out? How much more valuable is a man than a sheep!" (Matthew 12:10–12).
- When Jesus was asked by a rich man, "Good teacher,... what must I do to inherit eternal life?" Jesus discerned the question's intent and compelled the man to think about just who he was addressing, as he responded with the question, "Why do you call me good?" (Mark 10:17–18).

THE VALUE OF A GOOD QUESTION

Asking questions is a good way to answer an objection. Responding with a question sends several positive messages:

- *I value your opinion.* It opens the way for a dialogue instead of a monologue. Asking a question says, "Tell me what *you* think."
- *I'm not trying to cram something down your throat.* Asking a question takes the adversarial tone out of the picture. It says, "Let's compare what you think to what I think, and see if we can come to some mutual understanding."

- *I want to understand what you are really asking.* Asking a question communicates that you value the other person. It gives you the opportunity to put him or her on center stage—and incidentally on the hot seat. It allows you to understand what the real issues are before you begin to give an answer.

In *Finding Common Ground,* Tim Downs suggests that questions are one of the thoughtful Christian's best tools for dealing with objections. Questions are nonthreatening. They communicate humility. They allow people to discover truth for themselves—a much more powerful way to learn than merely listening to others. And they strongly suggest that we are open to questions in return, which communicates that our desire is not to push our beliefs but to engage in dialogue.[2]

Jason Dulle suggests using three types of questions: (1) questions of clarification: "What do you mean by that?" (2) questions of justification for one's beliefs: "How did you arrive at that conclusion?" and (3) questions of consideration: "Have you ever considered ...?"[3] Clarification questions allow us to understand a person's real concern so we don't misinterpret. They also challenge colleagues to consider thoroughly and express clearly what they want to say. Justification questions uncover what a person believes—his or her worldview and basic assumptions—and allow us to see the logic behind a person's beliefs. If people glimpse any logical inconsistencies in their beliefs, they may be willing to rethink an unreasonable position.

Campus Crusade staff member Randy Newman notes that sometimes people really don't want answers:

> There have been many times (far too many, I'm afraid) when I have given what I knew was a biblically accurate, logically sound, epistemologically watertight answer—only to see the questioner shrug his shoulders. Instead of moving him closer to salvation, my answer pushed him further away. Rather than engaging his mind or urging him to consider an alternative perspective, it gave him ammunition for future attacks against the gospel.[4]

Randy tells of an antagonistic young man who asked, "So, I suppose you think that people who don't agree with you, like all those sincere followers of other religions, are going to hell!"

Randy responded gently, "Do you believe in hell?"

The young man looked puzzled, perhaps because he was being intellectually challenged when he thought *he* was the one doing the challenging. Finally, after a long silence, he said, "No, I don't believe in hell. I think it's ridiculous."

Randy chose to echo the young man's own word choice. "Then why are you asking me such a ridiculous question?"[5] Randy was modeling one of Jesus' most common methods of planting — asking thoughtful, challenging questions.

Another student asked Randy, "Well, I *do* believe in hell. Do you think everyone who disagrees with you is going there?"

A great question. Possible responses: "Have I said something that makes you think people are going to hell just because they disagree with me?" or "Heavens, when it comes to truth, I could be as wrong as the next guy. How can we really find truth?"

Randy took another direction and asked, "Do you think anyone goes there? Is Hitler in hell?"

His questioner answered, "Of course Hitler's in hell."

Randy continued: "How do you think God decides who goes to heaven and who goes to hell? Does he grade on the curve?"[6]

From that point on, Randy said the discussion became civil for the first time, and they had some serious interaction about God's holiness, humanity's sinfulness, and Jesus' atoning work. Answering with questions turned out to be an effective way to share the gospel. But what do you think would have happened had Randy tried to press a point?

What if a coworker asks you how you explain God in light of the attacks on the World Trade Center? You could respond with a question: "That's a really good question. How would *you* explain it?" Or another person asks you why you believe in Jesus. You could give a long intellectual answer, or you could ask, "Have you read about him?" or "What do you know of his teachings?" or "What impresses you about his life?"

If a colleague asks if you believe all Muslims or Hindus are going to go to hell, you could quote Acts 4:12: "Salvation is found in no one else, for there is no other name under heaven given to men by which we must be saved." Or you could explain the difference between Islam or Hinduism and Christianity. Or you could ask, "What religion do you follow?" or "That's an interesting question. What makes you think I think that?" or "Have you studied the teachings of the Islam or Hindu religions?"

After I (Walt) became a Christian in college, Phil and I debated the creation-evolution issue for almost three years. At the end of our debate, he conceded the possibility of creation and admitted that evolution was a theory. Yet he still rejected Jesus. I had dinner with Phil about twenty years later. He still proudly declared his atheism. During dessert, he asked me to explain, from my Christian perspective, the role of disease in people's lives. I was tempted to teach—after all, I knew the arguments and the data. But thankfully I heard a gentle whisper say, "Ask and listen."

I breathed a prayer, asking for wisdom, and said, "Phil, from your viewpoint, how would you answer that question? How do you explain evil?"

Phil's eyes welled with tears. The issue was intensely personal. "Walt, I don't have an answer."

"Phil," I began, "can I tell you a story?" He nodded, and I told him about the anger Barb and I felt when we discovered that our first child had suffered severe brain damage. I told him about the lessons some loving Christian friends had taught us about disease and evil. And about how our marriage and faith had grown stronger through those dark days. It was a tearful conversation for both of us, with seeds planted for the hearing of the gospel. Although I don't see Phil often, when we do get together, our times are very special. And with each visit he has more questions—and so do I.

Don't misunderstand us. In many cases a simple answer to a direct question is the best response. Answering a question with a question can make you appear to be ducking the issue. But it can also open doors that no other method can unlock. Remember that people will find it hard to trust Jesus until they can first trust his messenger. So be sure to think before you rush through an open door about whether a direct response or a question is more appropriate.

TURNING OBJECTIONS INTO OPPORTUNITIES

How you handle objections, questions, or concerns determines whether they become opportunities or obstacles. As we have mentioned, an objection is sometimes, at least in part, a test. Coworkers may be attracted to your faith, but as you talk with them, an objection arises. Although the question or objection may seem like an attack, they may really be wondering, Are you going to blast me? or Do you really care about what I think? Are you like the other critical Christians I've met, or do you really care about me? or Do you have a reasonable answer that you aren't going to cram down my throat?

IMPORTANT GUIDELINES

It bears repeating: Answering objections is not about winning an argument. It's about building a relationship of trust, exchanging viewpoints without damaging the connection with a colleague. Making disciples is our core business. We need to filter everything we say and do through a grid that reflects this priority. When you face objections at any level, remember these guidelines:

Don't React Negatively

The first principle of turning objections into opportunities is to not react negatively. Instead, expect and even welcome objections and questions. The gospel can be hard to swallow—so don't be surprised if someone chokes on the truth when they confront it. Even though I (Bill) was raised in a church and never doubted the existence of God, I had trouble swallowing a key point of the gospel message, namely, that I deserved to be separated from God for eternity. I came at the issue from a human point of view, thinking that I was a pretty good person compared to a lot of other people. For me to resolve this issue, I had to look at it from God's point of view. The point is that I choked for a time on this issue. We should not be surprised when others choke, and we should not react negatively.

Don't Get Discouraged

Count on the fact that everyone has a soul hunger, even if someone turns up his or her nose at what you serve. The desire for meaning and purpose can't be self-manufactured or satisfied by oneself—or even by others. Ultimately, as Augustine said, our hearts are restless until they find rest in God. If someone is at least willing to talk with you about spiritual issues, be thankful that he or she is still "shopping," if not yet buying.

I (Bill) will never forget Jerry's final months as a non-Christian. He leveled every objection in the book at persons of faith who engaged him, including his wife. But he didn't run. And the closer he got to faith the more conflict he saw between his worldview and the Bible. Occasionally he'd get frustrated that we had reasonable answers for some of his questions or that we wouldn't get angry over an outlandish statement he made about what we believed. Looking back, I can see that he was becoming more anxious as the Holy Spirit closed in on him—until he finally came to trust Jesus.

Recognize the Value of Doubt

Doubt is often the doorway to faith—and it can be an indication that people are genuinely pondering an issue. Something is troubling them. If they never express their doubt, how will they ever find someone who can soothe their doubt? Give them an answer if you have one. Give them time and room to think. And give them respect. If they are comfortable expressing doubt to you, they probably trust you and feel safe talking to you—and that's a good thing!

If You Don't Know the Answer, Admit It

In an age that values authenticity, your honesty is as important as a good answer. When you admit you don't have all the answers, you level the playing field and enable a person to identify with you. If you don't know an answer, offer to research this question with them. By joining your coworkers in looking for answers, you may end up introducing them to other Christians. Remember that you're not called to be the "Bible answer man" for pre-Christians; you're called to love and serve them.

Don't Discount the Experience or Beliefs of Others

An attacking approach is rarely successful and will most likely cause hard feelings in the workplace. Don't try to correct every doctrinal inaccuracy you hear. God doesn't need you to be the resident theological police.

> I don't think there is any room for banging over the head. In this day and age where people think independently, and their culture reinforces that — doing that will drive people away.
>
> *Marvin N. Schoenhals,*
> *financial services*

The most powerful way to challenge people to reevaluate their beliefs is to ask them how their system is working. Is what they believe—what they are investing their life in—bringing them true joy and satisfaction? If it is, you can back off until they have a crisis or feel loneliness or dissatisfaction.

Whether now or later, you can help people get in touch with their deep longings. Rick Richardson suggests that our questions should disturb their souls and make them ask, "Does this life we're living make any sense?" Here are the kinds of issues Richardson suggests we consider raising:

- How should we feel about bringing our kids up without a moral anchor or rudder in a world that is drifting toward teen violence, sexual disease, and environmental disaster?
- How should we feel about a rootless tolerance that refuses to identify right from wrong?
- How should we feel about the belief that there is no right and wrong? Why should we get angry at corporate executives who profited by cooking their company's books?
- What sense does it make to support unrestricted sexual expression and unhindered efforts at self-fulfillment when we see the breakup of the family and the price our children are paying?[7]

Don't Treat Non-Christians Like the Enemy

How did Jesus deal with nonreligious nonbelievers? Always graciously. Although all of us are in rebellion against God, he doesn't treat us as we deserve: "For if, when we were God's enemies, we were reconciled to him through the death of his Son, how much more, having been reconciled, shall we be saved through his life!" (Romans 5:10).

Jesus recognizes that we are captives of a real Enemy, and we need to be set free. As he began his ministry, he proclaimed this loud and clear:

> The Spirit of the Lord is on me,
>> because he has anointed me
>> to preach good news to the poor.
> He has sent me to proclaim freedom for the prisoners
>> and recovery of sight for the blind,
> to release the oppressed,
>> to proclaim the year of the Lord's favor.
>
> Luke 4:18–19

Isn't it amazing how he deals with us? All of us still fall short of God's glory. We need to put our guns down and stop shooting at the people for whom Jesus died.

Turn an Objection into a Faith Story

A story from your life that paints a picture of how you struggled with whatever issue is at hand will go further than any good argument. It will give you credibility and increase the amount of trust your listener places in you.

Learn Some Answers That Defend the Faith

You don't have to have a PhD in theology. You don't even need to be a skilled apologist for the faith. But every Christian should know a few short, reasonable answers to give to the questions non-Christians ask. And we should know where to find answers to the questions others are asking. There are many excellent books available, such as I'm Glad You Asked by Ken Boa and Larry Moody; The New Evidence That Demands a Verdict by Josh McDowell; and The Case for Faith by Lee Strobel.8 The objections of non-Christians can be boiled down to about twelve basic questions, which are covered in I'm Glad You Asked. Search Ministries offers an audiotape series called "Search for Meaning," featuring a dialogue between a non-Christian and a Christian on some of life's big questions (available from Search Ministries, 1-800-617-3272):

How well can you answer these common questions asked by non-Christians?

Rate yourself from 1 to 5 (1 = I'm still asking that myself; 5 = I've got this one nailed)

____ 1.   How can I be sure God even exists?
____ 2.   Are miracles possible?
____ 3.   Isn't Christianity just a psychological crutch?
____ 4.   Is the Bible reliable?
____ 5.   If God is good, why do the innocent suffer?
____ 6.   Isn't it too narrow to say that Jesus is the only way to God?
____ 7.   Will God judge those who never hear about Jesus?
____ 8.   If Christianity is true, why are there so many hypocrites?
____ 9.   Can good works get us to heaven?
____ 10. Isn't "just believing" too simple?
____ 11. What does the Bible mean to *believe* in Jesus?
____ 12. Can anyone be sure they are going to heaven?

PRINCIPLES FOR TRUTH TELLERS

If you want to be a truth teller, learning and practicing the following principles will give you a strong foundation for making a difference wherever the Lord places you:

PRINCIPLE 1: USE THE BIBLE ITSELF WHENEVER YOU CAN

When you begin the process of planting, there is no more powerful tool than God's Word. Jesus said, "If you hold to my teaching, you are really my disciples. Then you will know the truth, and the truth will set you free" (John 8:31–32). The truth can come in many forms—my words, your words, or someone else's words. Certainly ideas, including our own ideas, can have both relevance and power. But there is something qualitatively different about the words of the Bible: "The word of God is living and active. Sharper than any double-edged sword, it penetrates even to dividing soul and spirit, joints and marrow; it judges the thoughts and attitudes of the heart" (Hebrews 4:12).

The International Bible Society puts it well:

God's Word
Gets under our skin.
Penetrates our hearts....
It invites.
Reveals.
Convicts.
And creates belief.[9]

Although your own words may be logical and true, we suggest that you use the Bible when establishing your side of the argument.

We're not suggesting that you beat people over the head with it. In fact, with some people if you pull out the Bible prematurely, they'll assume you can't think for yourself. To argue from the Bible with someone who doesn't respect its authority is like arguing from Marx to prove something to Alan Greenspan. But when people come to a point of genuinely

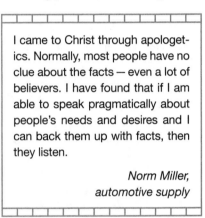

I came to Christ through apologetics. Normally, most people have no clue about the facts — even a lot of believers. I have found that if I am able to speak pragmatically about people's needs and desires and I can back them up with facts, then they listen.

Norm Miller,
automotive supply

searching for the truth, asking them to consider what the Bible says is the most powerful thing you can do.

When God's people, God's Spirit, and God's Word work together, the results can be truly miraculous.

PRINCIPLE 2: BALANCE TRUTH WITH GRACE

Why should we expect the world to be gracious to us when we haven't been gracious to others? Don't misunderstand. There is a time to speak out against blatant malevolence—to tell the truth about sin. But to those we are trying to reach, a lot of what passes for confronting sin in our culture looks like throwing stones. Grace calls for the kind of compassion that points people to the One who can meet their needs.

When we cast stones, the world has a right to get angry with us. We're assuming a role that neither our culture nor God has granted us the authority to take. Stone-throwing, according to Jesus, is the prerogative of the sinless. So none of us qualify. When the Pharisees brought an adulterous woman to Jesus, even he—the only sinless person ever to walk this earth—offered grace rather than condemnation (see John 8:11). Jesus models a crucial balance of truth and grace that will create awe rather than anger. While telling the truth ("Go now and leave your life of sin"), he offered grace ("Then neither do I condemn you").

PRINCIPLE 3: BALANCE KNOWLEDGE WITH HUMILITY

Graciousness toward others is a by-product of personal humility. The need to confront the beliefs or behaviors of others often has more to do with the immaturity, not the strength, of one's faith. A secure faith has nothing to prove and is willing to let a person travel to the truth at his or her own pace. Secure faith humbly extends grace because we know how desperately we need it ourselves.

> The Scriptures tell us to be of good repute with people within and outside the church. I try to pray to be winsome and kind and treat people right. Then you earn that respect that gives you an open forum. We try to have an attitude of treating people the way we want to be treated.
>
> Norm Miller,
> automotive supply

When it comes right down to it, "knowing the truth" can be pretty dangerous stuff. After all, abstaining from eating from "the tree of the knowledge of good and evil" was the one negative command given in Eden, and rightly so (see Genesis 2:17). Paul warns in his letter to the Corinthian church, "Knowledge puffs up, but love builds up. The man who thinks he knows something does not yet know as he ought to know" (1 Corinthians 8:1–2).

Knowledge without humility makes one arrogant; it misses the truth about others and about ourselves and our common need of grace. Knowing right from wrong does not make a person superior. A bit earlier in his letter Paul asks, "For who makes you different from anyone else? What do you have that you did not receive? And if you did receive it, why do you boast as though you did not?" (1 Corinthians 4:7).

The most compelling idea we have to impart is that the Lord Jesus, the Sovereign Ruler of the universe, loves all of us and wants to make new creations out of our broken lives. Jesus demonstrated he could be both tough on sin and compassionate to sinners. Interestingly, he reserved his most passionate reproach for the people who knew the Bible best, or at least thought they did. But for sinners Jesus has this welcome and endearing invitation:

> Come to me, all you who are weary and burdened, and I will give you rest. Take my yoke upon you and learn from me, for I am gentle and humble in heart, and you will find rest for your souls. For my yoke is easy and my burden is light.
>
> Matthew 11:28–30

Do those who are weary and burdened find us gentle and humble? If they don't, we may win an argument but end up losing their hearts, to say nothing of their minds and wills.

WHOM DO YOU LOVE?

When Congressman Steve Largent spoke at a prayer breakfast in Tennessee, he told of meeting Mother Teresa in 1996 at the time Congress awarded her with honorary American citizenship. Before she left the Capitol on that occasion, Largent and several colleagues asked her how they might pray for her. She told them to pray that her love for the poor would not eclipse her love for Jesus. Whatever cause may motivate us, let this be our prayer: that nothing would eclipse our love for Jesus and that nothing would ever interrupt his love for people, love that Jesus desires to flow through us to others.

THE BOTTOM LINE

Turn objections into opportunities by answering with grace and humility.

12

MAKING THE MISSION
POSSIBLE

Dave was a successful real estate developer in the Orlando area. He and I hit it off during a business organization. Over time, Barb and I became close friends with Dave and his wife, Ann. We traveled together, we took the kids to soccer games, and Barb and Ann led our daughters' scout troop.

We discovered that Dave and Ann had no spiritual upbringing to speak of and had had more than a few unfortunate encounters with aggressive, condescending, and hypocritical Christians. Dave especially was wary of Christians. In fact in retrospect, I find it amazing that he could have even been interested in a relationship with me. But the more we got to know each other, the more my spiritual faith—expressed by faith flags and faith stories—seemed to intrigue him.

After about a year, I gave my personal testimony to Dave over lunch one day. He listened with interest and asked questions. Eventually, he and Ann accepted an invitation to attend our home Bible study. Although Ann told Barb she was interested in a personal relationship with Jesus, she didn't want to take this step unless Dave did also. For months, I communicated the gospel to Dave in every way I could. I gave him books; we listened to and discussed tapes. But no matter what I did, the more I talked and the more questions I answered, the harder Dave's heart seemed to become.

Frustrated, I decided it was time to shake the dust off my feet (see Matthew 10:14) and invest less time with Dave and Ann. After all, there were other "interested pre-Christians" with whom Barb and I could spend time. To add to the frustration, Dave was purposely stalling a business deal. He said he couldn't make up his mind—

leaving me pretty much convinced that he wasn't going to make up his mind about anything.

I recounted my frustration to my spiritual mentor, Bill Judge, who asked a tough question: "Do you really care about these people, or are they just a project?" Sheepishly, I had to admit that getting them to make a decision to trust Jesus had become more important to me than being a friend. Bill asked another question: "How often do you and Barb pray for Dave and Ann?"

I hung my head. "I really don't pray for them very much at all."

He smiled. "They're making the toughest decision of their lives — and you can't make it for them. There is one important thing you *can* do, though, that will help them more than all the time and energy you've put into the relationship so far: pray for them."

When representing Christ to others, we must always examine our motives, making sure that the person we are trying to reach is someone about whom we care, and not just another "project." Even when our motives are right, we ultimately cannot control the results. The frustration I was experiencing with Dave is not uncommon for anyone who desires to see friends and associates come to faith in Jesus. It's even more frustrating if you've seen enthusiastic responses from others in the past. When you have developed a significant amount of trust, clearly explained the gospel, and answered most of a person's questions, you expect him or her to come to faith. It's exactly what *ought* to happen next, right? Jim Petersen has this helpful reminder:

> Probably the most dangerous thing about methods is that when they work, we begin to rely on them. We experiment with something. It works. We do it again, and again it works. As we become successful, we slip into thinking that continued success is a matter of just keeping that activity going.[1]

The battle of the will within a person's heart can delay his or her salvation for months or years. This is God's battle, not ours. A person has to make a decision only he or she can make, and the most important thing — and sometimes the only thing — we can do at this point is to pray, to cry out to the only one who can help, namely, God.

SOIL ANALYSIS

The volitional barrier to faith seems to be the toughest heart-soil challenge to overcome. By and large, Christians can gain the intellectual high ground. But that fact is irrelevant if people don't *want* to believe. Mark Twain summed it up pretty well: "It ain't the parts of the Bible I can't understand that bother me. It's the parts that I do understand."

The struggle to believe is brilliantly expressed by Arthur Krystal in an article titled "Why Smart People Believe in God" in Phi Beta Kappa's *American Scholar* journal:

> It's easy enough to understand why people want to believe, but actually to believe with one's whole heart and mind in divine grace — that to me is a true miracle.
>
> What's agitating me is religion envy, an unjustifiable resentment of intelligent and skeptical people — I almost said "people who ought to know better" — who swim effortlessly toward the sanctity of dry land, while others, like myself, spiritually adrift, seem unable to strike out for shore. I don't mind admitting that I'm flummoxed by their groundedness, their conviction, their serenity....[2]

Even though Krystal admits his envy of a Christian's peace, the undeniable pull of the love of a God willing to die for our sins, and the foolishness of preferring cynicism to experiencing God, he can't bring himself to believe:

> Still, you have to allow others the right of refusal; some can't or won't inhale transcendence. The biblical god is out of the question, not because of intellectual scruples but because of a temperamental predilection to go it alone.[3]

Wow! It's possible to understand and still not act on it. Being smart doesn't solve the problem if you're committed to absolute independence of will. Fundamentally, the human will, apart from God's help, is unable to respond to Jesus, who declared these words of truth: "No one can come to me unless the Father who sent me draws him" (John 6:44).

The volitional barrier is characterized by an unwillingness to change, no matter what, regardless of facts or feelings. In our spiritually dead condition, we are predisposed to resist examining spiritual issues or to reject Jesus outright. It's the response of a sinful, fallen nature. It's why men and women are unwilling to deal with sin. It's why many avoid exposure to the truth, refuse to risk, decline to trust anyone but themselves, and fear that which is unknown. Jesus said that "men loved darkness instead of light because their deeds were evil" (John 3:19).

Just as objects are bound to the earth by the force of gravity, the will is bound to the world by the force of sin. Human volition does not have the power to escape the gravitational pull of sin, much less to correct the soul's rebellious streak.

Paul observes that we all "followed the ways of this world and of the ruler of the kingdom of the air" (Ephesians 2:2). Apart from Jesus, worldly values and lifestyles trap every man and woman. As incompetent as the world is to offer true life, when men and women do a cost-benefit analysis of trusting Jesus, they face a dilemma: Their alternatives are to trust the temporal, which can be held and perceivably controlled, or to trust something beyond their control and their ability to quantify.

Here's the deal: When empty men and women develop life strategies that bring even a meager amount of satisfaction, it's hard to get them to look elsewhere. C. S. Lewis likens it to trying to get children from the slums to go on a beach vacation when they've never seen the shore:

> We are half-hearted creatures, fooling about with drink and sex and ambition when infinite joy is offered to us, like an ignorant child who wants to go on making mud pies in a slum because he cannot imagine what is meant by the offer of a holiday at the sea. We are far too easily pleased.[4]

Even assuming that someone would venture to step out of darkness into the kingdom of light, we can expect external resistance as well. As a person moves toward Jesus, a terrible battle with spiritual foes is being waged in the very heart of the person. Satan does not release his captives without a struggle.

THE SOIL TREATMENT

Indecision and love of the darkness result in pride and independence, which further isolate individuals from the truth. Left unchallenged, the human volition will never change course enough to avoid the inevitable path toward eternal destruction.

As we move through the phases of cultivating and planting and finally arrive at harvesting, the goals shift. In the earlier stages we sought to win an individual's trust. Once someone trusts us, he or she will begin to entertain the possibility of trusting what we say. But in the harvest phase, it's time for the individual to decide whether to put his or her trust in Jesus himself.

The only treatments we have at this stage are gentle persuasion that speaks to the will; meaningful discussion that continues to remove intellectual barriers; love, which continues to breach emotional walls; and prayer, which cries out to God for a person's salvation. The frustrating thing is that we can introduce a person to Jesus, but we can't compel him or her to become his friend.

LIFE AND DEATH DECISIONS

There are some striking parallels between health care and the spiritual life. Darlene was a patient of mine (Walt's) when I practiced in the rural Smoky Mountains. She did not trust doctors, and she especially did not trust hospitals. Everyone she knew who went to the hospital ended up dying. It was only because she was unconscious due to a life-threatening hemorrhage that an ambulance crew was able to get her through the hospital doors.

Once she arrived in our emergency room, with prayer and rapid action I was able to stop the hemorrhage. As Darlene recovered, she and her husband warmed up to me, and a bit of trust began to develop. When Darlene became pregnant, she returned to me for care. As she asked questions and learned about preventive medicine, she took better care both of herself and her unborn baby.

Sadly, one day Darlene discovered a lump in her breast. A biopsy confirmed she had cancer. I gave her the diagnosis, the prognosis, and the course of treatment. But she refused to accept treatment, convinced it would harm her baby. She was wrong in this assessment, but nothing we health care professionals could say or do would convince her otherwise. Before even seeing her baby's first birthday, she died.

I had been blessed to have won the trust of Darlene and her family. They listened to me intently as they considered the proposed treatment. They even gave intellectual assent that what I was saying was right. But when Darlene chose not to follow my potentially lifesaving medical recommendation, her decision led to her death.

Courtship and marriage provide another apt picture of this crisis of the will. A man and woman can be introduced, fall in love, and even discuss the possibility of marrying. But eventually they must make the decision to take the vows, sign the marriage license, and become husband and wife. Until they say "I do," they're not married.

It's easy to get frustrated with people like Dave and Ann, whose story we told at the beginning of the chapter. It's easy to forget that we're on *God's* courtship timetable. Rush a person's will—push for a decision—and there's a chance that the trust you've developed will be damaged and that you—or someone else—will have to start all over.

Judy Gomboll says, "Evangelism that ignores wooing and tries to force a union misses the very heart of the new life in and with Jesus Christ.... Give the Bridegroom plenty of time to do His courting!"[5] This is serious courtship, where Jesus appeals to *all* areas of our lives—the mind, the will, and the emotions—to embrace him. And mind, will, and emotions will all struggle together with this final decision.

A STRATEGY FOR THE BATTLE OF THE WILL

How do we face such challenges? While we ought always to be improving our skills to express our faith with grace, dealing with the will drives us back to what's ultimately important with regard to spiritual impact.

A FIRST-CENTURY SUCCESS STORY

The early church experienced phenomenal success as it spread the gospel. In some sixty years, the number of Jesus' followers grew from a few hundred on the day of Pentecost to over half a million by the end of the century. In a day that boasted no means of mass communication beyond the shout of the human voice, the gospel spread like wildfire, mainly person to person—men and women sharing the gospel with friends, relatives, acquaintances, colleagues, masters, slaves, students, teachers, customers, shop owners, and fellow soldiers.

But the success of the spread of the gospel was due to more than the mass mobilization of street-level Christians—even though that was key. It was also due, we believe, to the persistent pattern of prayer of the early church. They believed it was an absolutely essential component to their mission of carrying the message of Jesus to the ends of the earth. If ever there was someone who could have, by sheer force of personality, persuaded hosts of people to follow Jesus, it was the apostle Paul. And yet, we hear Paul echoing his cry for prayer throughout his letters (see Ephesians 6:19–20; Colossians 4:3).

Paul knew that without prayer the door to the human heart remained locked and bolted from within. When we trace throughout Acts the expansion of the early church, it's not surprising to see how this dependence on prayer played itself out. Rather than ask you to read through the book of Acts and highlight the instances of prayer (though this would be a worthy project), here's a short summary:

- As the early church waited for the promised Holy Spirit to bestow power to be Jesus' witnesses, "They all joined together constantly in prayer, along with the women and Mary the mother of Jesus, and with his brothers" (Acts 1:14).
- The apostles prayed for guidance as they sought a new colleague to replace Judas: "Then they prayed, 'Lord, you know everyone's heart. Show us which of these two you have chosen'" (Acts 1:24).
- After Pentecost, prayer was a key activity of Jesus' followers in Jerusalem: "They devoted themselves to the apostles' teaching and to the fellowship, to the breaking of bread and to prayer" (Acts 2:42). It's no wonder that this devotion brought forth an incredible revival in Jerusalem: "And the Lord added to their number daily those who were being saved" (Acts 2:47).

- When Peter and John were released after their first arrest, the church prayed: "When they heard this, they raised their voices together in prayer to God.... And they were all filled with the Holy Spirit and spoke the word of God boldly" (Acts 4:24, 31).
- Prayer was so important to the success of the church that the apostles refused to let anything get in its way. When food distribution to widows became a pressing concern, they brought everyone together and said, "It would not be right for us to neglect the ministry of the word of God in order to wait on tables. Brothers, choose seven men from among you who are known to be full of the Spirit and wisdom. We will turn this responsibility over to them and will give our attention to prayer and the ministry of the word" (Acts 6:2–4).
- As the church moved beyond Jerusalem, prayer was key to the joy and freedom the gospel brought to Samaria: "When the apostles in Jerusalem heard that Samaria had accepted the word of God, they sent Peter and John to them. When they arrived, they prayed for them that they might receive the Holy Spirit" (Acts 8:14–15).

As the narrative of Acts continues and focuses its attention on Paul, the most persuasive evangelist of the early church, we find the same emphasis on prayer. It's not surprising to find Paul on his knees immediately after his dramatic conversion on the road to Damascus (Acts 9:11). Prayer was the pattern of the disciples' ministry (Acts 9:40; 10:9). The gospel came to the first Gentile believers—the Roman centurion Cornelius and his family—in response to prayer (Acts 10:30–31). When Peter was thrown into prison for preaching the gospel, the church prayed and saw his miraculous release (Acts 12:5). Before the church at Antioch sent Paul and Barnabas out to spread the gospel through what is now Turkey, they prayed (Acts 13:3). Before Paul and Barnabas took leave of the new believers in a town where they had ministered, they prayed (Acts 14:23). The gospel was first taken into Europe in response to the prayer of God-seeking women in Macedonia (Acts 16:13). When Paul and Silas were thrown into prison for proclaiming Jesus, they prayed (Acts 16:25). Before Paul left the followers of Jesus in Ephesus and Tyre, he spent time with them in prayer (Acts 20:36; 21:5). Paul prayed for his captors to come to believe in Jesus (Acts 26:29). And the last miracle in the book of Acts was empowered by prayer: "[Publius's] father was sick in bed, suffering from fever and dysentery. Paul went in to see him and, after prayer, placed his hands on him and healed him" (Acts 28:8).

A MODERN NECESSITY

Prayer is just as essential today. What we say about God to people is only as effective as what we say about people to God. Why is prayer so important to evangelism? As Jesus said to his disciples, "Apart from me you can do nothing" (John 15:5). J. Sidlow Baxter once said, "Men may spurn our appeals, reject our message, oppose our arguments, and despise our persons, but they are helpless against our prayers." After all is said and done, our task is to cry out to God to draw a particular person to himself.

With all the modern tools and strategies at our disposal, it's easy to become obsessed with media, methods, and techniques. But wonderful tools though they are, they are just that—tools. And they are useless if not empowered by the Master through prayer. In many ways we have advantages that far exceed what the early church possessed, but in reality we have no more power than they did. We have less, in fact, if we fail to pray.

PRAYER IN THE WORKPLACE

A few years ago, a business owner asked me (Bill) if it was all right to pray for his business. I was startled that this man—someone who was very sincere about his faith—had no idea how much God cared about his business. If we are going to experience God's power in our work, prayer at and for the workplace must be habitual—especially if we want to see coworkers take incremental steps of faith toward a relationship with Jesus.

PRAY FOR YOURSELF

Given that we are unable to accomplish anything of spiritual significance without Jesus working through us (see John 15:1–17), prayer for ourselves is critical. In praying for ourselves, we should ask that

- we would do excellent work that attracts others' attention (Proverbs 22:29).
- our work would bring glory to God (Matthew 5:16).
- we would treat people fairly (Colossians 4:1).
- we would have a good reputation with unbelievers (1 Thessalonians 4:12).
- others would see Jesus in us (Philippians 2:12–16).
- our lives would make our faith attractive (Titus 2:10).
- our conversations would be wise, sensitive, grace-filled, and enticing (Colossians 4:5–6).
- we would be bold and fearless (Ephesians 6:19).
- we would be alert to open doors (Colossians 4:3).
- we would be able to clearly explain the gospel (Colossians 4:4).
- God would expand our influence (1 Chronicles 4:10).

Pray for Others

The apostle John notes that if we ask anything according to God's will, God hears us (1 John 5:14). My (Walt's) mentor encouraged me to pray the following petitions for Dave and Ann. Based on these Bible passages, we recommend that you pray seriously for your pre-Christian friends that

- the Father would draw them to himself (John 6:44).
- they would seek to know God (Deuteronomy 4:29; Acts 17:27).
- they would believe the Bible (Romans 10:17; 1 Thessalonians 2:13).
- Satan would be restrained from blinding them to the truth (Matthew 13:19; 2 Corinthians 4:4).
- the Holy Spirit would convict them of sin, righteousness, and judgment (John 16:8–13).
- God would send other Christians into their lives to influence them toward Jesus (Matthew 9:37–38).
- they would believe in Jesus as their Savior (John 1:12; 5:24).
- they would turn from sin (Acts 3:19; 17:30–31).
- they would confess Jesus as Lord (Romans 10:9–10).

- they would yield their lives to follow Jesus (Mark 8:34–37; Romans 12:1–2; 2 Corinthians 5:15; Philippians 3:7–8).
- they would take root and grow in Jesus (Colossians 2:6–7).
- they would become a positive influence for Jesus in their realm (2 Timothy 2:2).

Barb and I began to pray every day for Dave and Ann. We continued to cultivate and plant and share. We continued to love them. Our friendship grew—as did our time on our knees, bathing the relationship in fervent prayer.

> My prayer list has a lot of people I work with on it. I don't know where they all are spiritually, but I pray for them because they are part of our organization. I pray for my entire organization, and for my senior leadership group by naming each one of them.
>
> *Marvin N. Schoenhals,*
> *financial services*

Nearly seven years after the start of our relationship, we saw God answer these prayers. Dave and Ann both decided to become followers of Jesus. With some for whom we've prayed, the wait has been only days; for others, it has been decades. Yet we wait in hope, and we pray.

To keep us praying regularly, both Bill and I keep a list of unbelieving people for whom we pray. We encourage you to do the same.

It's important to be discreet with prayer. Some people are offended to know they are the subject of prayer. Keep your list confidential; if you keep it on your computer or PDA, keep it password-protected. Be very cautious about emailing requests for prayer for other people to Christians in your company, even if this kind of personal use is permitted. Email messages have great potential to be misrouted. If people begin to hear that a group is praying for them—and they haven't asked for it—at the very least they'll feel like an outsider, and at worst they may be highly offended. Take the same precautions for group prayer. Confidentiality is essential.

Pray with Others

If your faith has an attractive quality to it, you will, somewhere along the line, undoubtedly have the opportunity to pray with the people you work with. Sometimes they will ask for prayer; sometimes they'll seek help with a need or problem. If your company doesn't see it as a misuse of your time, and the person is agreeable, praying together on the spot can be a powerful experience for a nonbeliever who is seeking help. Otherwise, promise to pray later. Be sure to check with the person periodically to see how God is at work to meet the need.

In whatever form it takes, prayer is the force that moves the hand of God. Years ago my (Bill's) father gave me a small, tattered book he'd had for forty years. The wise words of E. M. Bounds changed the trajectory of my spiritual influence on others. Bounds writes, "We are constantly on a stretch, if not a strain, to devise new methods, new plans, new organizations to advance the church and secure enlargement and efficiency of the gospel."[6] Bounds goes on to say that while we are looking for better methods, God is looking for better people—praying people. He's right. Prayer is what moves the Hand that moves the human heart to faith and makes our mission possible.

> Often one of our management staff or an employee will want to talk to me about a personal issue. Quite honestly, they are issues that are so deep there is nothing I can do for them. But I can pray for them. I can sincerely ask God to come into their lives and to help them. I can't tell you the number of times when we've closed the door and I have prayed hand in hand with individual staff members. I find it so interesting — the impact this has. They'll come back later and say that it was a turning point in fighting the battle.
>
> *Larry Collett,*
> *information technology*

THE BOTTOM LINE

Evangelism is a process—a long process—that depends more on prayer than on anything else we do.

THE START-UP

Our discussion of evangelism has included several parallels with the business world. We want to make one last analogy: Evangelism is a lot like starting a new company. There's much more work on the front end than you can ever imagine. And once you get things going, new companies—as well as new believers—need nurturing and attention. They need help to grow and develop.

Jesus' last instructions to his disciples were to make *disciples*, not just believers, implying that there is something for the body of Christ to do after someone crosses the line of faith in Jesus: "Go and make disciples of all nations, baptizing them in the name of the Father and of the Son and of the Holy Spirit, and teaching them to obey everything I have commanded you. And surely I am with you always, to the very end of the age" (Matthew 28:19–20).

Make no mistake, a man or woman who is involved in the harvest has a responsibility to see to it that a new believer receives spiritual care after salvation, just as parents have the responsibility to see that their newborn child is nurtured and cared for. This doesn't mean you have to be a spiritual "family physician," providing total care. It means that you help someone get started, that you find the men and women he or she needs to come alongside to help him or her grow into a fully developed, mature follower of Jesus.

Comparing the church to a body, the apostle Paul reminds us that each of us has a part to play or a work to do to help others come to Jesus and then to go on and grow in their relationship with him: "From [Christ] the whole body, joined and held together by every supporting ligament, grows and builds itself up in love, as each part does its work" (Ephesians 4:16). Paul teaches that everyone has gifts needed to help the body of Christ grow. The purpose of apostles, prophets, evangelists, pastors, and teachers (see Ephesians 4:11) is to prepare or equip God's people to use their gifts to help each other grow up spiritually.

So to raise a spiritual infant, it takes a church—a group of believers who, as they speak the truth in love, foster growth in Jesus.

DEVELOP A PLAN

According to the Small Business Administration, "Starting and managing a business takes motivation, desire, and talent. It also takes research and planning. Lack of planning is one of the leading causes of business failures."1 As you cultivate and plant in faith, planning ahead will become natural. As you foresee the kind of spiritual start-up a person will need after a spiritual birth, consider the following questions:

- What do I have that can contribute to a person's spiritual growth?
- What specific things can I teach?
- How much time do I have available to spend with him or her?
- With what other concerned Christians does this person already have a relationship?
- To what other caring Christians can I introduce this person?
- What other resources are needed for this person's spiritual growth?
- What books or resources that I've read would help this person get started in a new spiritual life?
- Which church would be most helpful for this particular person?
- What kind of gifts could this person bring to the body of Christ?

FACE THE OBSTACLES

As you help a person begin a spiritual journey from salvation to maturity, you will face obstacles—many of which are the same ones you faced in helping a person come to faith in Jesus.

TIME

Instinctively we know that helping a new Christian grow requires a serious time investment on someone's part. No one has the gifts or the time to do it alone. And all too often, when one person attempts it, discipleship becomes more of a spiritual cloning procedure than developing the person into the unique child of God he or she was meant to be.

If you've been working as a team in the process of evangelism, why not consider the same approach during discipleship? Everyone can pitch in by providing what he or she does best. If a person has been attending a nurturing church during the seeking part of his or her journey, all the better. A host of people and opportunities can be marshaled to help the new Christian grow in faith. But don't assume you can abandon "your spiritual baby" on the doorsteps of the church, turning the responsibility over to the spiritual professionals. Remember Ephesians 4? Pastors and teachers are *not* to do the ministry of discipleship alone but equip others in the body of Christ for the work of serving others.

SELF-DOUBT

Even if you are a fairly mature believer yourself, you may wonder what you have to offer someone else. You may still have gaps in Bible knowledge or in understanding what it means to walk with Jesus daily. You may also feel that your personal struggle with sin disqualifies you from helping someone else.

Despite your limitations, you still have something to offer. You *are* gifted to do something. Don't let what you can't do keep you from doing what you can. Other Christians can play a key role here in affirming that you have something important to offer to others spiritually. Let self-doubt move you toward growth.

SETBACKS

As you prepare to nurture new Christians, realize that the reality is not always going to match your hopes. We'd all love it if people kept making steady progress with Jesus, never taking a backward step. But it just isn't the case. New believers experience setbacks morally, spiritually, and emotionally—as do more mature believers. Almost every Christian we've ever worked with experienced doubts about what they committed to when they came to faith in Jesus, and whether they are truly forgiven and accepted by God. Was it real? Is

Jesus real? Does God really love me? Have I lost my salvation? Am I making this up to make myself feel better? Was I really sincere? If I'm still struggling with sin, am I really God's child?

RECOGNIZE THE PROCESS OF GROWTH

As we look at our own lives, it becomes clear that no one's soil is perfect. All of us have rocks and weeds. If we struggled with lust, greed, or anger before our spiritual birth, we may continue to struggle with these temptations after we choose to follow Jesus. The difference is that now we have a new life in us and a power that can help us change.

At the point of salvation, God does miraculously deliver some people from the power of some sins. But for many, these temptations follow across the line of faith and torment them until they learn to believe that they really do have the power to say no to sin.

For most new believers, the process begins with intentionally focusing their *minds* on the spiritual realities of their new identity in Christ: "Since, then, you have been raised with Christ, set your hearts on things above, where Christ is seated at the right hand of God. Set your minds on things above, not on earthly things. For you died, and your life is now hidden with Christ in God" (Colossians 3:1–3).

Then they have to choose with their *wills* to obey God and act in a way that corresponds to who they really are:

> Put to death, therefore, whatever belongs to your earthly nature: sexual immorality, impurity, lust, evil desires and greed, which is idolatry. Because of these, the wrath of God is coming. You used to walk in these ways, in the life you once lived. But now you must rid yourselves of all such things as these: anger, rage, malice, slander, and filthy language from your lips. Do not lie to each other, since you have taken off your old self, with its practices and have put on the new self, which is being renewed in knowledge in the image of its Creator.
>
> Colossians 3:5–10

Lastly, they must go on to confront their *emotions* with the truth about their new identity:

Let the peace of Christ rule in your hearts, since as members of one body you were called to peace. And be thankful. Let the word of Christ dwell in you richly as you teach and admonish one another with all wisdom, and as you sing psalms, hymns and spiritual songs with gratitude in your hearts to God.

Colossians 3:15–16

In no way do we want to minimize sin and its impact on our lives. But rather than wallowing in shame, we can let our mistakes stimulate us to grow. Be careful, then, not to heap shame on new converts. The Holy Spirit is still in charge of the cleanup. Help them understand the power of God, and let the Holy Spirit do his work. Expect the best, because that's what is possible in Jesus. Don't be surprised at the worst, though, because spiritual growth is a process.

Depending on the type of baggage, some people need skillful, Bible-based counseling and healing prayer to unplug the power of past pain and hurt before they can experience God's power. Some need correction and the assurance of both God's love and our love. Some need to learn to overcome negative self-talk. Some need help with fear or guilt or lack of trust in God. Some need a nudge and others need a shove to wake them up to the reality of what they are doing to others and themselves. And all of us need a growing understanding of who God has made us to be in Jesus Christ.

MINIMUM DAILY REQUIREMENTS FOR SPIRITUAL GROWTH

Some years ago, the Food and Drug Administration developed a chart that showed the essential foods needed daily to maintain health. The battle still rages, though, over what constitutes the healthiest diet. It's no surprise that many of us are confused about physical nutrition. But there's no excuse for being confused about what we need to grow spiritually. The Bible doesn't give us specific "menus" for experiencing God's grace in our daily lives, but it does clearly indicate the kind of spiritual diet we need.

This spiritual nurture is evident in the church's early days as described in Acts 2:42–47. We see five core experiences mentioned in this passage:

- experiences of learning God's Word
- experiences of responsible involvement in serving others
- experiences of worship through knowing and responding to God
- experiences of community with other followers of Jesus
- experiences of evangelism as we pass on the grace we've been given

These experiences outline the diet that will help new believers grow toward maturity. I (Bill) have pictured these experiences like this:

These experiences are interdependent. Each one influences and enriches the others. For example, something you learned about God in a Bible study can come to mind during a worship service and become the basis of praise.

These experiences are not chronological. Although they can be approached systematically, there is no fixed order or priority in which these key experiences must be encountered. In other words, a person might take *responsibility* to volunteer in a ministry or talk to nonbelieving friends about Jesus (*evangelism*) before he or she chooses to be involved in an intentional *learning* experience.

These experiences are also not isolated. Core experiences can occur simultaneously. Someone may experience *learning* as well as *community* through a small group Bible study, or he or she may experience *community* in a ministry volunteer team (*responsibility*).

Acts 2:42–47 will serve as our framework for examining each of these spiritually nutritional "food groups."

EXPERIENCES OF LEARNING

In his description of the Jerusalem church, Dr. Luke points out right off the bat that the church was engaged in learning together: "They devoted themselves to the apostles' teaching" (Acts 2:42). They intentionally tried to learn more about God, his Word, and his world.

Learning Begins with the Truth

Jesus declared, "If you hold to my teaching, you are really my disciples. Then you will know the truth, and the truth will set you free" (John 8:31–32). For faith to grow, a new believer must come to know God's Word. Faith is only as solid as the truth on which it rests. Because the Bible can be confusing to novices, you may want to suggest a Bible study for them to join. If they don't have a modern translation of the Bible, give them one, marking the meaningful verses you used to communicate the gospel.

Truth Must Be Applied and Obeyed

The accumulation of biblical knowledge is not the goal. Knowledge will remain lodged in the head, never penetrating the heart, unless a new believer translates this knowledge into faith by *acting* on what he or she knows. And once the truth is applied and obeyed, it will produce faith. Faith is something that develops as we respond to the truth. Knowledge translates into faith when we take a risk that what we have learned in theory may actually be true in reality. Like a muscle, every time we exercise faith, our faith becomes stronger. As we risk, we meet God in our circumstances and find him to be everything we hoped him to be. Theory never becomes reality in our lives, though, without practice.

EXPERIENCES OF RESPONSIBILITY

The Christian life is one of faith that expresses itself in active service to others. The apostles weren't the only followers of Jesus involved in active ministry in the early church: "All the believers were together and had everything in common. Selling their possessions and goods, they gave to anyone as he had need" (Acts 2:44–45).

Everyone is a player on the team. The Jerusalem believers were actively serving one another, meeting physical, spiritual, and emotional needs. Our job in the body of Christ is to serve. There's just no way to justify staying in the stands when God is calling you to play. God has given everyone a contribution to make. Even though some would say that a new believer should spend time "being" rather than "doing," we would argue for balance. When we emphasize one over the other, both sides lose. Getting new Christians involved in the giving of themselves in service is important to their spiritual growth and development.

EXPERIENCES OF WORSHIP

If Satan succeeds in keeping new followers of Jesus confused about God, he will control their lives and succeed in corrupting their faith. That's why worship is so important. Acts 2:46–47 tells us that the church "continued to meet together in the temple courts. They broke bread in their homes and ate together with glad and sincere hearts, praising God."

Worship Begins with Knowing God

A reporter once asked Albert Einstein's wife if she understood the theory of relativity. She replied, "No, but I know Albert, and he can be trusted." We can say the same thing about God.

It's tempting for us to think of God as someone we go to only when we need to be rescued from some trouble. We cannot afford to worship the god we *want*, then keep him on the shelf until we have a problem and need to summon him. We must worship the God who *is*—the God who has revealed himself in the pages of Scripture and in the flow of history.

As we begin this adventure of knowing and praising God for who he is, we can be sure that Satan will do everything he can to thwart our attempts, trying to direct our worship to some lesser god. C. S. Lewis captured the evil intent of the demonic world in his book *The Screwtape Letters*. Demon Screwtape, in an instructional letter to an apprentice tempter, notes, "Whatever the nature of the composite object, you must keep [the young Christian] praying to it—to the thing that he has made, not to the Person who has made him."[2]

Worship Involves Responding to God

Worship is a contraction of two words—*worth* and *ship*. To worship is to ascribe worth or give value befitting the object of worship. Worship involves our words, to be sure. Each Sunday, men and women gather in churches to "ascribe worth" to God in song and prayer. But worship involves much more than words spoken with deepest sincerity of heart. Worship is also what a Christian does with his or her life. It involves words and deeds expressed in response to who God himself is: "And whatever you do, whether in word or deed, do it all in the name of the Lord Jesus, giving thanks to God the Father through him" (Colossians 3:17). We are to live our lives as an act of worship.

Our lives are a response to who we believe God to be. He is either the Sovereign Master of the universe who deserves our absolute attention, obedience, and enjoyment, or he is an illusion of a more manageable deity—a god we can contain in our minds and who has a hard time attracting our attention away from more interesting things.

EXPERIENCES OF COMMUNITY

God is our ultimate refuge. But he also chooses to provide a tangible place of safety—a "hope and strength franchise" on earth—by means of the church. In Acts 2, we see the church sharing life together:

> All the believers were *together* and had everything in common. Selling their possessions and goods, they gave to anyone as he had need. Every day they continued to meet *together* in the temple courts. They broke bread in their homes and ate *together* with glad and sincere hearts.
>
> Acts 2:44–46, emphasis added

Together is the operative word. These Christians' lives, activities, and possessions were interwoven. By community, we're not talking about a worship gathering where you sit in a pew and watch a performance. Community happens in a group of people who are mutually committed to one another. Every new believer needs a community of other believers to encourage and help him or her grow.

Community satisfies so many of our longings. It provides encouragement, reminding us that we are safe even in the midst of excruciating pain. When we remind one another of God's love and commitment, we give hope. Community provides a setting where all believers can be urged to do the right thing—to stand, resist, endure, hang tough, make the hard choices, and choose God's best. When we remind each other of who God is, who he has made us to be, and how he wants us to live, we stand as God's representatives who lend strength to the resolve of a new brother or sister who may be weak.

Several years ago, George's business was sailing through troubled waters. On a trip to the West Coast, he ran across an incredible opportunity involving the distribution of soft-core pornographic videos. After a night of serious wrestling, he called the person who had offered the opportunity and said no. The next Thursday at his small group, he told us the story. He said, "You all know I need the money but not bad enough to do something wrong. My relationship with God is too important to me." And then he added, "I would have made a different decision two years ago before I joined this group."

Community also provides the setting in which appreciation and affirmation can be mutually shared. Showing appreciation to a new follower of Jesus for making a contribution breathes life into a heart that may be discouraged. We stand in God's place as we remind new Christians that God wants to use them for great and mighty things. When we affirm others, it communicates that we value them for who they are. Affirming someone shows that we accept him or her without demanding change but still encouraging improvement. When we affirm others' value by our words or actions, we stand in God's place as we remind them of the unconditional love and commitment they now have in Jesus.

Finally, community enhances health. In my (Walt's) book *10 Essentials of Highly Healthy People*, in a chapter titled "Avoid

Loneliness," I discuss the many medical studies showing that the social support provided by a loving community increases the quality and length of life.[3] Dozens of studies from around the world indicate that healthy relationships matter and that loneliness can kill.

Psychologist Larry Crabb wisely points out, "We need a place to admit and explore our desires, a community of fellow journeyers who believe that our desires are not shameful but thoroughly human and already met in Jesus."[4] New believers need vital relationships with other people with whom they can discuss the dilemmas of life.

EXPERIENCES OF EVANGELISM

When men and women take God seriously, study his Word, do his work, and are committed to their spiritual brothers and sisters, outsiders notice. No wonder we read, "And the Lord added to their number daily those who were being saved" (Acts 2:47).

We don't need to say a lot more about evangelism in a book about evangelism, but there is a key principle to keep in mind with regard to new Christians: *Every new believer is a witness*. Nothing should stand in the way of new followers of Jesus becoming involved in evangelism. No, they don't know everything. Yes, it may be dangerous for them to spend time with non-Christian friends. But we were born to reproduce spiritually, and the sooner we get started, the better.

We believe Charles Spurgeon had it right: The way you defend the Bible is the same way you defend a lion—you just let it loose. Even though new believers may not be the most skilled witnesses, they still are witnesses. Even if all a new believer can say is "Look at what Jesus did for me," it can have a powerful impact. Consider the Samaritan woman (John 4). She was just barely in the kingdom herself and already was telling others about Jesus. The blind man healed by Jesus (John 9) testified in a simple but powerful manner to what had happened to him. He didn't understand all the theology, but he knew what he had experienced.

And don't forget that new believers can be such powerful witnesses because Jesus is the only treasure they have—and they know it. With one foot out of the spiritual grave, they feel a major connection with those who are lost.

Just like new companies, newborn believers need attention and nurturing. As men and women come to Jesus, grow in their commitment to studying his Word, take responsibility to serve others, respond in worship to who they know God to be, develop a community to live their lives authentically, and begin to give away their faith, they have the spiritual capital they need to establish their faith and to flourish.

THE BOTTOM LINE										
Salvation is just the beginning of eternal life.										

An Eternal Impact
One Life at a Time

As we began this book, we proposed four simple but big ideas:

- Evangelism is a process. The journey of faith takes place over the course of time as a person makes many small, incremental decisions that lead to the big decision of trusting and following Jesus.
- Our job in evangelism is to discover where God is already at work in a person's life and to join him there, not to force a conversation or persuade someone to pray a prayer he or she may not be ready to pray.
- Being a person of spiritual influence is every Christian's calling, not just the responsibility of a gifted few.
- More so than the inside of a church building or a foreign mission chapel, the workplace is the most strategic place of ministry for most Christians.

We hope you've caught a vision for how you can make a difference in the men and women working around you—one life at a time. More than ten years ago, we accepted a challenge put forward by Os Guinness in a little booklet called *Winning Back the Soul of American Business*. He identified a conundrum and a challenge inherent in the American situation in the 1990s:

> The conundrum lies in the fact that American business is close to the heart of both the American crisis and the necessary answer to that crisis. The challenge lies in the fact that far too few business leaders have recognized the nature of the problem and far too few Christian leaders have stepped forward to offer a constructive response.

But is the situation ... beyond the capacity of individuals and small groups to effect decisive change? Emphatically not. America has yet to see the consequences of strategic initiatives carried forward by leaders whose business prowess is matched by their faith, vision, and resolve.[1]

"The Saline Solution," written for medical professionals, was our first "constructive response" to communicate what we were learning about workplace evangelism. In *Workplace Grace*, we've taken the biblical principles that proved so helpful and inspiring to medical professionals and translated them for the general workplace. We hope you've been inspired to take up the challenge, individually or as a group.

If you still doubt what God can do through you—just one solitary person—consider the following passages of Scripture:

> The eyes of the LORD range throughout the earth to strengthen those whose hearts are fully committed to him.
>
> 2 Chronicles 16:9

> Go up and down the streets of Jerusalem,
>   look around and consider,
>   search through her squares.
> If you can find but *one person*
>   who deals honestly and seeks the truth,
>   I will forgive this city.
>
> Jeremiah 5:1, emphasis added

> I looked for *a man* among them who would build up the wall and stand before me in the gap on behalf of the land so I would not have to destroy it, but I found *none*.
>
> Ezekiel 22:30, emphasis added

> If you remain silent at this time, relief and deliverance for the Jews will arise from another place, but you and your father's family will perish. And who knows but that *you* have come to royal position for such a time as this?
>
> Esther 4:14, emphasis added

If you doubt what God can do through you—just one solitary person—consider the remarkable life of William Wilberforce. Born into a life of careless privilege in the mid-1700s, coming to faith in Jesus in his mid-twenties, Wilberforce considered leaving his post in parliament to pursue theological studies. Challenged by John Newton to consider that God could have a purpose for him where he was, Wilberforce remained in public service. In his diary on October 28, 1787, he wrote, "God has set before me two objects, the suppression of the Slave Trade and the reformation of manners."[2] Rarely has an individual made a more audacious statement. The abolition of the slave trade involved bringing to a halt an economic enterprise that placed millions of pounds sterling into the British economy. The reformation of manners involved the transformation of the moral culture of his day.

Three days before Wilberforce's death on July 26, 1833, the bill for the abolition of slavery passed its second reading in the House of Commons. And by the end of the nineteenth century, goodness and justice and other Christian virtues had become fashionable in contrast to the loose morality and corrupt public life of the late 1700s. Rarely has the power of one individual life been so poignantly demonstrated.

Yet a closer look at Wilberforce's life reveals that he in no way worked alone. A network of friends and fellow followers of Jesus—a spiritual strategic alliance—encircled Wilberforce and joined their energy to his. This group included fellow members of parliament, neighbors, a royal prince, a duke, a marquis, and the famous potter Josiah Wedgwood. Together these men and women operated like "a meeting which never adjourned"[3] as they pursued change in society and also in individuals.

As we've seen, spiritual impact can begin with something as simple as having a cup of coffee with a colleague or listening compassionately to a customer. It can also include doing something that goes above and beyond the call of duty. Fancy techniques and memorized strategies are not required to share the love of Jesus. We don't need to be the office piranha, poised to pounce on unsuspecting souls at the watercooler with a gospel tract. Small actions and simple efforts to serve others in the course of everyday work have a bigger impact than the "spiritual intrusions" we often attempt out of guilt.

The early church did not depend on professional evangelists. Those doing the first-century work of evangelism were not themselves evangelists. They were the nameless thousands who followed Jesus without fanfare or notoriety. Even the apostles were quite ordinary men. Before they were biblical heroes, they were someone's neighbor trying to make a living as best they could. They were street-level men with a noble mission that moved them beyond their fears and beyond themselves.

Because ordinary people shared the gospel with their colleagues, customers, and clients, the early church grew to more than half a million believers in less than seven decades. If men and women in the workplace seize the spiritual opportunities they have and work together, could we see the church grow a thousand percent, as happened in the first-century church? Only the Lord of the harvest knows. But when you take your call seriously to talk about your faith publicly, God will bless your efforts in ways immeasurably beyond all you can ask or imagine. Who knows what extraordinary things God will do with the ordinary moments in the workplace that you give to him?

This is our prayer for you: "Whatever you do, whether in word or deed, do it all in the name of the Lord Jesus, giving thanks to God the Father through him" (Colossians 3:17).

THE BOTTOM LINE									

You, working within the body of Christ, can make an eternal difference in the lives of your coworkers.

NOTES

CHAPTER 1 SPIRITUAL ECONOMICS

1. "News: Wal-Mart Stores at a Glance" (available at http://www. walmartstores.com/wmstore/wmstores/Mainnews).
2. George Barna, *Evangelism That Works* (Ventura, Calif.: Regal, 1995), 127.
3. "Unchurched People" (available at http://www.barna.org/cgi-bin/Page-Category.asp?CategoryID=38).
4. Barna, *Evangelism That Works*, 58.
5. Cited in K. C. Hinckley, *Living Proof: A Small Group Video Series Discussion Guide* (Chattanooga, Tenn.: Christian Business Men's Committee and the Navigators, 1990), 29.
6. This chart was adapted from *Living Proof: A Small Group Video Series Discussion*, 27, and James F. Engel and Wilbert Norton, *What's Gone Wrong with the Harvest?* (Grand Rapids: Zondervan, 1975), 45.
7. Win and Charles Arn, *The Master's Plan for Making Disciples* (Grand Rapids: Baker, 1998), 45–46.
8. Arn and Arn, *The Master's Plan for Making Disciples*, 46.

CHAPTER 2 CALLED TO THE WORKPLACE

1. Dorothy Sayers, *Creed or Chaos?* (Manchester, N.H.: Sophia Institute Press, 1995), 76–77.
2. Sayers, *Creed or Chaos?* 77.
3. Quoted in John Fischer, *What on Earth Are We Doing?* (Ann Arbor, Mich.: Servant, 1996), 85.
4. Sayers, *Creed or Chaos?* 77.
5. Robert Slocumb, *Maximize Your Ministry* (Colorado Springs: Nav-Press, 1990), 247–49.

CHAPTER 3 IS ANYONE HUNGRY?

1. George Barna, *Evangelism That Works* (Ventura, Calif.: Regal, 1995), 22.
2. Barna, *Evangelism That Works*, 72.
3. United States Census 2000 Summary File (SF–3)—Sample Data, Table QT-P16.
4. Diane Schmidley, *Profile of the Foreign-Born Population in the United States: 2000*, U.S. Bureau of the Census, Current Population Reports, Series P23–206, (Washington, D.C.: GPO, December 2001), 3.

5. United State Census 2000, "Frequently Asked Questions" (available at http://www.census.gov/dmd/www/genfaq.htm).
6. Barna, *Evangelism That Works*, 35–36.
7. Barna, *Evangelism That Works*, 23, 34–35.
8. Walter L. Larimore and William C. Peel, *The Saline Solution* (Bristol, Tenn.: The Paul Tournier Institute, 1996), 19.
9. Barna, *Evangelism That Works*, 72.

CHAPTER 4 EARNING THE RIGHT TO BE HEARD

1. Cited in Robert Banks and Kimberly Powell, eds., *Faith in Leadership* (San Francisco: Jossey-Bass, 1999), 39.
2. Carlton Snow, "Rebuilding Trust in the Fractured Workplace," in Banks and Powell, *Faith in Leadership*, 39.
3. Snow, "Rebuilding Trust in the Fractured Workplace," in Banks and Powell, *Faith in Leadership*, 43.

CHAPTER 5 KEEP IT SIMPLE

1. Tom Peters, *The Circle of Innovation* (New York: Knopf, 1997), 460.
2. Cited in Peters, *The Circle of Innovation*, 468.
3. Barna, *Evangelism That Works*, 73.
4. John Fischer, *Fearless Faith* (Eugene, Ore.: Harvest House, 2002), 196.
5. Fischer, *Fearless Faith*, 198.
6. Fischer, *Fearless Faith*, 198.
7. Robert Snyder, "Lessons Learned on the Journey" (30 March 2001); to subscribe to "Lessons Learned on the Journey," log on to www.pursuantgroup.com/ihs/subscribe.

CHAPTER 6 FOSTERING CURIOSITY

1. Sarah E. Hinlicky, "Talking to Generation X," *First Things* 90 (February 1999): 11.
2. Religion News Service, "Jars of Clay: Humanity Is Frail," *The Orlando Sentinel* (22 November 1997).

CHAPTER 7 BUILDING STRATEGIC ALLIANCES

1. Cited in Isabel M. Isidro, "Small Businesses and the Power of Strategic Alliances," *Add Me Newsletter*, Issue 208 (12 June 2001), on the Web at http://www.addme.com/issue208.htm.
2. Paul Brand, MD, "The Challenge of Evangelism for the Medical and Dental Professions," ed. Leonard W. Ritzman, MD, *Evangelism for the Medical and Dental Professions* (Dallas, Tex.: The Christian Medical and Dental Society, n.d.), 21.

3. See Acts 2:42–43; 1 Corinthians 12:26–27; Ephesians 4:15–16.
4. See Acts 11:20–26; 13:2–5; 15:39–16:5.

CHAPTER 8 EVANGELISM BY WALKING AROUND

1. Peters, *The Circle of Innovation*, 4.
2. Cited in Oren Harari, *The Leadership Secrets of Colin Powell* (New York: McGraw-Hill, 2002), 33.
3. Cited in Harari, *Leadership Secrets of Colin Powell*, 38.
4. Cited in Harari, *Leadership Secrets of Colin Powell*, 201.
5. Tom Peters and Nancy Austin, *A Passion for Excellence* (New York: Random House, 1985), 9.
6. Peters and Austin, *Passion for Excellence*, 32.

CHAPTER 9 HOW TO WALK THROUGH AN OPEN DOOR

1. Marian R. Stuart and Joseph A. Lieberman, *The Fifteen Minute Hour: Practical Therapeutic Intervention in Primary Care*, 3d ed. (Philadelphia: W. B. Saunders, 2002), 85–86.

CHAPTER 10 THE WHOLE TRUTH

1. You may want to have booklets available that use a modern translation or paraphrase, such as a copy of "The Message of Hope" from *The Message* (available from NavPress—call 1-800-366-7788; http://www.navpress.com/message.asp) or *The Great News: Gospel of John* in the New International Version (available from International Bible Society—call 1-800-524-1588; http://www.gospelcom. net/ibs/).
2. Rick Richardson, *Evangelism Outside the Box* (Downers Grove, Ill.: InterVarsity Press, 2000), 129–40.
3. George Barna, *Evangelism That Works* (Ventura, Calif.: Regal, 1995), 107–25.
4. Barna, *Evangelism That Works*, 116.

CHAPTER 11 FACING OBJECTIONS

1. This list of responses (as well as the preceding one) is taken from "Heart for the Harvest" seminar manual (Fort Worth, Tex.: Search Ministries, 1991,) 54–55.
2. Tim Downs, *Finding Common Ground* (Chicago: Moody, 1999), 129–30.
3. Jason Dulle, "The Question of Truth and Apologetics in a Modern/ Postmodern World" (available on the Web at http://www.apostolic. net/biblicalstudies/apologetics.htm).

4. Randy Newman, "Stop Answering Questions: the right questions can open the door to spiritual dialogue," *Discipleship Journal* 127 (January/February 2002): 25.
5. Newman, "Stop Answering Questions," 25–26.
6. Newman, "Stop Answering Questions," 26.
7. Adapted from Richardson, *Evangelism Outside the Box*, 93.
8. Ken Boa and Larry Moody, *I'm Glad You Asked: In-depth Answers to Difficult Questions about Christianity* (Colorado Springs: Victor, 1995); Josh McDowell, *The New Evidence That Demands a Verdict* (Nashville: Nelson, 1999); Lee Strobel, *The Case for Faith* (Grand Rapids: Zondervan, 2000).
9. "The Truth of God, the Truth of Us," Scripture Catalogue (Colorado Springs: International Bible Society, 2002), 2–3.

CHAPTER 12 MAKING THE MISSION POSSIBLE

1. Cited in Hinckley, *Living Proof: A Small Group Video Series Discussion Guide*, 95.
2. Authur Krystal, "Why Smart People Believe in God," *American Scholar* (Autumn 2001): 69.
3. Krystal, "Why Smart People Believe in God," 78.
4. C. S. Lewis, *The Weight of Glory* (New York: Collier, 1980), 3–4.
5. Judy Gomboll, "Matchmaker! Matchmaker!" *Discipleship Journal* 57 (May/June1990): 28.
6. E. M. Bounds, *Power Through Prayer* (Grand Rapids: Baker, 1972), 5.

CHAPTER 13 THE START-UP

1. "The Facts About ... Starting a Small Business" (http://www.sba.gov/gopher/Business-Development/General-Information-And-Publications/obd1.txt).
2. C. S. Lewis, *The Screwtape Letters* (New York: Macmillan, 1968), 21–22.
3. Walt Larimore, MD, *10 Essentials of Highly Healthy People* (Grand Rapids: Zondervan, 2003), 135–55.
4. Larry Crabb, *The Safest Place on Earth* (Nashville: Word, 1999), 130.

CHAPTER 14 AN ETERNAL IMPACT ONE LIFE AT A TIME

1. Os Guinness, *Winning Back the Soul of American Business* (Washington, D.C.: Hourglass Publishers, 1990), 3.
2. Cited in John Pollock, *A Man Who Changed His Times* (Burke, Va.: The Trinity Forum, 1996), 11.
3. Cited in Pollock, *A Man Who Changed His Times*, 7.

Share Your Thoughts

With the Author: Your comments will be forwarded to
the author when you send them to *zauthor@zondervan.com.*

With Zondervan: Submit your review of this book
by writing to *zreview@zondervan.com.*

Free Online Resources at
www.zondervan.com

Zondervan AuthorTracker: Be notified whenever your favorite
authors publish new books, go on tour, or post an update
about what's happening in their lives at www.zondervan.com/
authortracker.

Daily Bible Verses and Devotions: Enrich your life with daily
Bible verses or devotions that help you start every morning
focused on God. Visit www.zondervan.com/newsletters.

Free Email Publications: Sign up for newsletters on Christian
living, academic resources, church ministry, fiction, children's
resources, and more. Visit www.zondervan.com/newsletters.

Zondervan Bible Search: Find and compare Bible passages in
a variety of translations at www.zondervanbiblesearch.com.

Other Benefits: Register yourself to receive online benefits
like coupons and special offers, or to participate in research.

ZONDERVAN®

ZONDERVAN.com/
AUTHORTRACKER
follow your favorite authors